CHARLES & DIANA
THE FIRST FIVE YEARS

Produced and Designed by
SERGE LEMOINE

Text by
ASHLEY WALTON

Photography by
JAYNE FINCHER

SCOTT PUBLISHING

First published in Great Britain 1986 by Scott Publishing
Company Limited, London, England.

Text: Scott Publishing Company Limited, 143 Fleet Street,
London, EC4Y 2BP, England.

Consultants: Jenny Flavill, Chris Walters.

Colour separations by Latent Image, London, England.

Typesetting by Spectrum Typesetting Ltd., London,
England.

Printed and bound by Collins, Glasgow, Scotland.

SCOTT PUBLISHING COMPANY LIMITED

CHARLES & DIANA
– THE FIRST FIVE YEARS

Contents

PICTURE ACKNOWLEDGEMENTS

Cover:	JAYNE FINCHER
Back Cover:	TIM GRAHAM
BBC Hulton Picture Library:	36-37. 43. 48-49. 50-51. 52-53. 54-55. 56-57. 58-59. 60-61. 62-63. 68-69. 70-71. 80-81. 88-89.
Camera Press:	38-40. 41. 72-73. 74-75. 76-77. 78-79. 148-149. 150. 206-207. 208-209. 273 (bottom). 274-275. 282-283. 284-285.
Tim Graham:	33. 178-179. 180-181 (top). 182-183. 272-273 (top). 276-277. 278-279. 280-281. 286-287. 288.
Press Association:	39.
Jayne Fincher:	*All remaining pictures.*

Royal Line of Succession

CERDIC, first king of the West Saxons
(d. 534)

Crioda

CYNRIC (534-560)

CEAWIN (560-591)

Cuthwine (d. 584)

Cuthwulf

Ceolwald

Cenred, under-king of Sussex (692)

Ingild (d. 718), brother of King Ine

Eoppa

Eaba

Ealhmund, under-king of Kent (786)

EGBERT = Redburh

ETHELWULF = Osburh (1st wife)

ALFRED THE GREAT = Ealhswith

EDWARD = Edgiva (3rd wife)

EDMUND I = Elgiva (1st wife)

EDGAR = Elfrida (2nd wife)

ETHELRED II THE UNREADY = Elfleda (1st wife)

EDMUND II IRONSIDE = Ealdgyth

Edward Atheling the Exile = Agatha

St. Margaret = Malcolm III of Scotland

WILLIAM I = Matilda of Flanders
(the Conqueror)

HENRY I = Matilda (1st wife)

Geoffrey, Count of Anjou = Matilda

HENRY II = Eleanor of Aquitaine

JOHN = Isabella of Angoulême (2nd wife)

HENRY III = Eleanor of Provence

EDWARD I = Eleanor of Castile (1st wife)

EDWARD II = Isabella of France

EDWARD III = Philippa of Hainault

John of Gaunt = Katharine Swynford   Edmund = Isabel of Castile
Duke of Lancaster   (3rd wife)   Duke of York   (1st wife)

John, Marquess of Dorset = Margaret Holland   Richard, Earl of Cambridge = Anne Mortimer

John, Beaufort, Duke of Somerset = Margaret Beauchamp   Richard, Duke of York = Cecily Neville

Edmund Tudor, Earl of Richmond = Margaret Beaufort   EDWARD IV = Elizabeth Woodville

HENRY VII = Elizabeth of York

James IV of Scotland = Margaret Tudor   HENRY VIII = Anne Boleyn (2nd wife)

James V of Scotland = Mary of Lorraine   ELIZABETH I

Mary, Queen of Scots = Henry Stuart, Lord Darnley (2nd husband)

JAMES I = Anne of Denmark

Frederick, King of Bohemia = Elizabeth Stuart

Ernest Augustus, Elector of Hanover = Sophia

GEORGE I = Sophia Dorothea of Celle

GEORGE II = Caroline of Brandenburg = Anspach

Frederick Lewis, Prince of Wales = Augusta of Saxe-Gotha

GEORGE III = Charlotte of Mecklenburg-Strelitz

Edward, Duke of Kent = Victoria of Saxe-Coburg-Saalfeld

VICTORIA = Albert of Saxe-Coburg and Gotha (Prince Consort)

EDWARD VII = Alexandra of Denmark

GEORGE V = Mary of Teck

GEORGE VI = The Lady Elizabeth Bowes-Lyon

QUEEN ELIZABETH II = The Prince Philip, Duke of Edinburgh

Charles, Prince of Wales   The Princess Anne   The Prince Andrew   The Prince Edward

Prince William   Master Peter Phillips

Prince Henry   Miss Zara Phillips

Britain's Sovereigns

William I	1066-1087
William II	1087-1100
Henry I	1100-1135
Stephen	1135-1154
Henry II	1154-1189
Richard I	1189-1199
John	1199-1216
Henry III	1216-1272
Edward I	1272-1307
Edward II	1307-1327
Edward III	1327-1377
Richard II	1377-1399
Henry IV	1399-1413
Henry V	1413-1422
Henry VI	1422-1461
Edward IV	1461-1483
Edward V	1483
Richard III	1483-1485
Henry VII	1485-1509
Henry VIII	1509-1547
Edward VI	1547-1553
Jane Grey	1553
Mary I	1553-1558
Elizabeth I	1558-1603
James I	1603-1625
Charles I	1625-1649
Commonwealth Declared 1648	
Oliver Cromwell Lord Protector	1653-1658
Richard Cromwell Lord Protector	1658-1659
Charles II	1649-1685
James II	1685-1689
William III and Mary II	1689-1702
	1689-1694
Anne	1702-1714
George I	1714-1727
George II	1727-1760
George III	1760-1820
George IV	1820-1830
William IV	1830-1837
Victoria	1837-1901
Edward VII	1901-1910
George V	1910-1936
Edward VIII	1936
George VI	1936-1952
Elizabeth II	Succeeded 1952

Today's Royal Line of Succession

1 H.R.H. The Prince of Wales (Heir Apparent)
2 H.R.H. Prince William
3 H.R.H. Prince Henry
4 H.R.H. Prince Andrew
5 H.R.H. Prince Edward
6 H.R.H. The Princess Anne
7 Master Peter Phillips
8 Miss Zara Phillips
9 H.R.H. The Princess Margaret
10 Viscount Linley
11 Lady Sarah Armstrong-Jones
12 H.R.H. The Duke of Gloucester
13 The Earl of Ulster
14 Lady Davina Windsor
15 Lady Rose Windsor
16 H.R.H. The Duke of Kent
17 The Earl of St Andrews
18 Lord Nicholas Windsor
19 Lord Frederick Windsor
20 Lady Helen Windsor

WONDERFUL FOR YOU

ALL THE WORLD LOVES A LOVER

H E TOOK his first glance at her beside the altar and whispered; "You look wonderful." "*Wonderful for you!*" replied his bride, thinking that this, at least, was one intimacy they could keep from the 750 million people watching their marriage vows: but they forgot the ancient art of lip-reading, which stole away even this snatch of loving small-talk at the beginning of their married life.

The world had just said hello to two young lovers, and the commoner who turned into a Princess at 11.15 on the morning of Wednesday July 29, 1981, sang for joy the moment her cathedral ordeal ended and her open carriage began to clatter back to the Palace where she would one day be Queen. The only song she could think of was the jingle to a popular television commercial. So, as a million people lining the streets of London cheered, Diana, the new Princess of Wales, sang: "*Just one cornetto, give it to me, delicious ice cream from Italy*".

And, as the swaying carriage gathered pace, the Royal Couple rolled back in laughter together on the leather seats as they reminded one another that Diana would always be remembered as the bride who forgot her husband's name. She called him Philip Charles, rather than Charles Philip, when she made her wedding vows.

Straight after that mistake, Prince Charles, the nervous groom, said, "All thy goods with thee I share," rather than, "All my *worldly* goods with thee I share," and the embarrassed memory of that, faithfully reported by the lip reader, had the Prince holding his sides. "Good God! Did I really say that?" he exclaimed.

Was this the same shy girl who, for five months of her courtship, peeped at the Press cameras from under her blonde fringe and who, 72 hours before her wedding, ran weeping from a public polo match? Diana didn't cry at her wedding, but the groom did: a tear sparkled on Prince Charles' cheek, matching one of his wife's diamond ear rings (borrowed from her mother) as the organ of St Paul's crashed out his favourite opening hymn "*Christ is Made the Sure Foundation.*"

The clear blue eyes of the schoolgirl who had set her cap at marrying the Heir to the British

Crown as she stood in the middle of a ploughed English field one November morning in 1977, stayed dry. The restless nervous energy she had displayed in the lead-up to the wedding had stripped more than a stone from her 5ft 10in frame, and now this once well-rounded former Sloane Ranger, whose idea of a quiet evening was curling up in front of a television soap opera with a packet of wine gums and a cup of instant coffee, resembled a top model with a tiny waist that looked as small as her Welsh gold wedding band. The girl the world's Press labelled "Shy Di" had gone forever.

This love affair sounds too romantic for words…more like a fairy-tale fantasy than anything approaching real life; a Once-Upon-A-Time tale of a handsome Prince, the most sought after bachelor in the world, suddenly noticing, with a jolt, the Cinderella next door, a schoolgirl with the puppy fat still clinging to her, who had blossomed into a beauty. And a plot liberally sprinkled with coincidences almost too far-fetched to be believed: a casual meeting at a polo match, a shared joke on the deck of the world's most luxurious yacht, a cheek to cheek dance at a glittering ball…

ALL THIS, followed by the laughter they shared turning to love one chilly morning as they strolled beside a salmon river in the grounds of an ancient Scottish castle the Prince would one day inherit; a proposal over a candlelit dinner for two in the Palace where he will be King, and a cathedral ceremony watched by the world and destined to go down in history as the wedding of the century.

That story unfolded in reality in front of a world that loves a lover. Their joy was plain to see, but what is amazing is how this couple failed to fall in love earlier. All her life she was there, right under his feet, quite literally the girl next door…but Prince Charles never seemed to meet Lady Diana Spencer or even notice her existence until one cold and wet November morning when they were introduced by Diana's sister, herself an old flame of the Prince, the Royal with a ladykiller reputation.

He fell in love in the autumn of 1980 and Diana, still an unworldly teenager, was catapulted into public life with all its attendant pressures.

It was a dramatic upheaval for a girl barely out of school to be swept up in the majesty of Royalty.

There was their first night together in a splendid country house under the romantic canopy of a four-poster bed; their love and excitement aboard the world's most luxurious yacht which took them cruising around the Mediterranean…14 days of pure enchantment. The Royal honeymoon which went on and on, but turned from perfect harmony to disharmony, as the pressures of being a Princess got to Diana and almost wrecked this match. She suffered and worried and Charles too became anxious as her weight dropped further and her health began to suffer.

It was then that the Royal Family rallied round, helping her to pull through so that what emerged from the trauma was a confident and trend-setting woman in her own right.

She recovered, to give birth to two bouncing baby Princes and take in round the world tours with Charles, developing together a social conscience as they both saw the problems facing the world today, especially inner city violence and drug addiction. They have both vowed to fight for a better world and, quietly behind the scenes, tried to use their influence to change things.

Before he married, Prince Charles said; "I hope I will be as lucky as my parents. I am forming a partnership which I hope will last 50 years. That is what marriage is all about."

The first five years have revealed that the people have a conscientious, well-intentioned, dedicated couple as their future rulers. Britain is lucky to have them. This then is Charles and Diana's first five years.

ROYAL HONEYMOON

ON A SUN-KISSED GREEK ISLAND

LESS THAN 12 hours after the wedding Prince Charles slipped the matrimonial hook and went fishing – alone! Diana had landed her Prince Charming but had yet to change his bachelor ways. Charles, as more than a few former girlfriends had found out to their cost, was what feminists of that period were calling an MCP (male chauvinist pig). He left his bride in the Portico Room in their lace-canopied king-sized, feather-filled four-poster and headed for the River Test, which ran through the 600-acre Broadlands estate, their honeymoon hideaway in Hampshire. "He didn't have much luck, there were no salmon," said water bailiff Bernard Aldridge, the man who gave away the Prince's slightly selfish attitude towards his new bride.

It was two hours before he returned to the Portico Room at Broadlands, once the stately home of the late Lord Louis Mountbatten. Her bridegroom's absence would not have gone without mention from Diana, the first Royal bride to choose to omit the word "obey" from the marriage vows. The next five years would see a subtle change in the Heir to the Throne, the man who once gloried in his bachelor role and was

nicknamed "action man," the hunting, shooting hard-riding, deep-diving and high-flying playboy Prince. Within three years Diana was to turn Charles into a family man, preferring the nursery, the living-room fire and his vegetable plot to those former antics.

The first task Diana set herself in her mission to change Charles began even before the wedding. Charles had always been a conservative dresser, Savile Row pinstripes, colourless ties, plain black lace-up shoes and never a pair of jeans, at least not in public anyway. Diana bought him, to the dismay of the Royal valet, trendy shirts from multiple tailors, brighter silk ties, extremely fashionable boxer shorts, and the Prince's first pair of slip-on shoes. His suits began looking just a shade more fashionable, and suddenly the Prince of Wales became much more aware of his appearance. But one area where the Princess failed is in his refusal to be seen in public in casual clothes: even when he accompanies her to pop concerts he still insists on shirt and tie. There is many a Press photographer who dreams of the day when the future King finally bows to his wife and turns up in public in blue jeans!

Broadlands, after the Princess managed to

drag her husband away from the elusive salmon, became an idyllic and romantic spot for the newlyweds, just as it had for the Queen, then Princess Elizabeth, and Prince Philip after their wedding on November 20, 1947. Charles and Diana strolled hand-in-hand across the lawns and enjoyed intimate dinners by candlelight as they chuckled over videos of their own wedding day which had been rushed down to Hampshire by special messenger.

A couple of days later the two of them flew off on the most exciting part of the Royal honeymoon. The 307 strong crew of the Royal Yacht Britannia took them off round the Mediterranean on a magical mystery tour designed, successfully as it turned out, to throw the world's Press off the scent. Britannia, more like a small liner than the common idea of a rich man's plaything, had been used by two other pairs of Royal honeymooners, Princess Margaret and Lord Snowdon in 1960 and Princess Anne and Captain Mark Phillips in 1973.

The world's most sought-after newlyweds foxed the Press in the great honeymoon hunt. While the clamouring reporters and photographers spent a small fortune following a carefully laid trail scattered with phoney clues, the Britannia steamed towards the Algerian coast, then veered away for Sicily and through the Straits of Messina and into the Ionian Sea. There at last the couple found peace on a sun-kissed Greek island of gods and legends.

They discovered a secret cove which could only be reached by boat, and there, under a brilliant blue sky and with temperatures in the 90s, Princess Diana swam in a bright yellow bikini as her husband sunbathed on the beach.

It was an enchanted fourteen days. The Prince and Princess spent most of their evenings alone on the Royal deck. Diana used the Queen's bedroom as her dressing room – it even had a double bed, the only one on Britannia, hastily winched aboard before sailing from Portsmouth to pick up the Royal couple in Gibraltar. No one on the yacht, except the official Royal Navy photographer, had been allowed to bring a camera. Even the four members of Prince Charles' personal staff were given official warnings "no cameras." Of course the rule didn't apply to Charles and Diana and the Princess spent a lot of time clicking away with her auto focus taking views of the Greek islands and pictures of her Prince.

While the Prince slept in the heat of the day the Princess, wearing only a skimpy wrap over a teeny weeny red biniki, wandered the maze of corridors chatting to everyone she met. Spotting Diana in her bikini became the major preoccupation of the lower decks. Sometimes the sailors would lower the steps so that everyone on board could swim in the sea. Crewmen swam at one end while the Princess splashed away at the other end of the yacht.

BRITANNIA'S OFFICERS invited the couple to a moonlight barbeque on a Greek island, and Diana and Charles joined in for an impromptu beach, camp-fire sing-song. Diana didn't forget the lower decks either. She surprised everyone by strolling into the other ranks area one day and, spotting a piano, insisting on another sing-song which could be heard over half the ship. On the last night at sea, with Charles as brown as new shoe leather and Diana sporting an enviable movie star tan, the crew held a farewell cabaret for the honeymooners. One large sailor dressed up as Lady Diana Spencer, complete with see-through skirt, and the Princess, remembering the embarrassing incident when photographers captured for posterity Lady Diana's fine pair of legs outlined under her thin cotton skirt, roared with laughter.

Diana's young dresser, Evelyn Dagley, the only other woman aboard, scampered on to the makeshift stage, carrying a large piece of cardboard covering her skimpy bikini, making her look completely naked. The sailors cheered with delight, and even the two Scotland Yard detectives on board danced on stage in their swimming trunks. The party lasted well into the early hours and the sailors' jokes got saltier and saltier, but the Princess loved it and laughed the night away.

The honeymoon lasted nearly three months, but the surroundings, exchanging the warmth of the Mediterranean for the damp chill of autumn Scotland, weren't exactly romantic. Charles had taken his bride to Royal Deeside to continue his honeymoon with the rest of the Royal Family who were holidaying at Balmoral Castle, exactly as he had spent Septembers all his life. The Royals have a set routine, Christmas at Windsor Castle, New Year at Sandringham in Norfolk and summer in Scotland, and he saw no reason for change.

The long honeymoon was a sensible idea, to get the fledgling Princess used to being part of the world's top Royal Family and adapt to being married before being pushed into public service.

It was to give Diana a chance to relax and enjoy married life before the goldfish bowl opened up to swallow her again in front of the all-seeing television cameras and the incessant Nikon motor drives. Buckingham Palace advisers knew that cameramen were now getting desperate for new pictures of this girl who had suddenly become a top pin-up, replacing models and film stars as the world's most photographed face.

In Balmoral, although the couple had some privacy from the rest of the family, staying at Craigowan, a house on the Royal Estate, there were lots of things the Prince could do…fishing, he loved that; stag stalking, he loved that too. All that fun combined with a little grouse shooting and some fine walking and riding – it was his idea of an outdoor paradise. The problem was that Diana didn't share her husband's love of the great outdoors. She was happier hunting on the concrete pavements of Sloane Street and Knightsbridge. Unlike the rest of the horse-mad Royals she hated riding; a childhood fall had given her a phobia of horses. So while the Prince enjoyed himself his bride became bored and depressed.

SOME sections of the media were beginning to say that the honeymoon had been going on too long. The world was anxious to see the beautiful Princess again. But in reality it wasn't just a couple of priviliged people having an extended honeymoon. There was another reason too for the two of them hiding away in the Scottish heather for so many weeks.

It was only since the wedding that they had actually got to know each other. Their courting was conducted largely in the presence of hundreds of journalists, and their private meetings were much in the manner of back-door, over-the-fence-type trysts accompanied by the clatter of milk bottles and dustbins lids. What with that and the internationally acclaimed spectacular of the wedding, the long honeymoon, on the drawing board at least, seemed to be a worthwhile idea.

Charles had one or two official outings, and attended the funeral of President Sadat, an event not in his diary. Otherwise they lived the life of Royal Riley at Craigowan, the home about 150 yards from Balmoral. Diana was able to pop down to London to do some shopping and see friends, but it was not a pleasant experience because she found for the first time that being a Princess means you just can't wander those Knightsbridge pavements alone any more. If Diana wanted to shop at Harrods she needed to take her personal armed Scotland Yard man plus two police back-ups in a following car. She had discovered what life in the Royal goldfish bowl would be like, and quite simply, it terrified her.

The Queen, though delighted with her new daughter-in-law, was also worried for her. Others too in the Royal Family were aware of what was happening to the young Princess. Friends, like the Prince's skiing chum Charles Parlmer-Tompkinson and Diana's old flatmates Carolyn Pride and Virginia Pitman, were invited up to Scotland to keep the Princess company.

Diana was also undergoing an indoctrination course in the leisurely art of depriving nature of its livestock as her husband shot, stalked and fished. However, love turned a blind eye to cruel death and the discomforts of sitting on a soggy windswept river bank watching her spouse cast the waters for several hours without so much as stirring a salmon from its slumbers.

But by this time the problems were beginning to build up. Diana had swapped from being immature, carefree, unknown teenager to a heavily protected married Princess overnight. She felt the eyes of the world were on her as she hid away in Scotland surrounded by the crackle of the police walkie-talkies and security men. The pressures on this young woman about to step out into public life were enormous. Diana was facing an immensely traumatic period and there were many, even inside the Royal Family itself, who feared she would not be strong enough to win through.

A DIFFICULT TIME

WHEN A FANTASY BECAME REALITY

"THAT FIERCE light which beats upon a throne," is how Tennyson described the pressures of Monarchy, and he was writing long before the advent of the popular Press, radio and television. How much harsher is that light when its principal target is a 20-year old girl who is about to become a mother.

The Fairy Princess lovingly portrayed by the mass media, digging ruthlessly through her past and declaring her to be a virgin, writing about her beauty and peering at her through telephoto lenses as if she were the latest inmate at London Zoo, was, all too obviously, only flesh and blood.

The first sight of the Princess of Wales on a rainswept quayside at Aberdovey in Wales came as a tremendous shock to the men and women of Fleet Street, still pursuing the myth of Diana. In just over a year she had been plucked from obscurity to become the most photographed woman in the world. But her vulnerability to this mass voyeurism was horribly apparent on that chill morning in Wales. It was the first chance to see Diana close up after the long honeymoon, and it was like looking at a different woman.

She had lost weight before the wedding; that was only to be expected...but the girl moving through the Aberdovey crowds, shaking hands and accepting flowers, wasn't slim, she was painfully thin. Her skin looked transparent; she looked terrible.

Diana commanded the finest services that money and prestige could buy. She was the envy of countless millions round the Globe, but what the young Princess needed at that particular time in her life was a period of calm. That she couldn't have as she began to learn the art of belonging to the most written-about family in the world. She was taking lessons from Prince Charles on how to meet her people and the spotlight was on her once again.

A few months before the wedding Diana had a problem with her figure. Although no one dared tell her, it was quite noticeable that the future Princess of Wales was slightly overweight. The seams of the vivid blue silk two-piece suit she wore for her engagement day photographs with her fiance were, to say the least, a little stretched. Diana, who was then a rounded girl with a full bosom, knew she would have to go on a diet. When she started refusing breakfast and only picked at her food as she dined with the rest of the Royal Family or at the formal banquets where she was one of the guests of honour, it did not go unnoticed.

There were genuine fears inside Diana's own family that this sort of crash dieting would lead to disaster. Diana's auburn haired older sister, Sarah, had once suffered from anorexia nervosa, the so-called slimmers' disease, when she was Diana's age, and Diana's mother was determined not to let that happen to her.

Diana had become very close to her mother during the engagement; there had always been a remarkable similarity between them. They looked alike, they were the same height (five feet ten inches) and build, and both became engaged in their teens to glamorous men. Her mother told her that her weight would fall away before the wedding simply because of the pressures alone. The pounds did melt, so much that the seamstresses fitting her for the wedding dress began to be worried about how much they were having to take in.

To make doubly sure of a svelte shape, Diana began taking exercise classes inside Buckingham Palace. A woman came in to play the piano and the future Princess would tap dance to its rhythm dressed in a series of brightly coloured leotards. Buckingham Palace footmen were told to keep away from that area of the Palace when Diana was dancing to save any embarrassing encounters between servants and the scantily-clad Royal fiancee.

But now it appeared to many journalists that the Princess, who as the former more rounded Lady Diana Spencer looked terrific in a photograph had gone too far in her desire to achieve a model girl's figure. Over the next few months the new look Diana began to spark off stories that she was suffering from anorexia, like Sarah. It was not true, but there was genuine concern inside the Royal Family for her health, and fears that the strain of adapting to life in the Royal Family might be too much for her.

Their first year of marriage wasn't all champagne and roses. For Diana, between the happiness and joy, there was pain and heartbreak. She was an unworldly girl plucked from her shared Earls Court flat and part-time job at the kindergarten, and thrown up as an object of mass adulation. People were waiting to see how she would cope.

Her close friends say she set out to capture the Prince of Wales – and succeeded. At first neither of Diana's parents wanted her to marry a man twelve years her senior. There were worries that hers was a schoolgirl fantasy she was playing out. The stress built up and it began to show, both in the weight loss and in bouts of tears and temper. Diana had always been a strong willed, although even-tempered girl, who expected her own way. When she did not get it she could be very difficult.

Suddenly, the honeymoon, a real-life fantasy of marriage with a handsome Prince, a beautiful yacht and constant admiration, became husband and wife reality.

"Nobody told me it would be like this!" The shout echoed clearly across a bleak and cold field swept by the freezing winds from the nearby North Sea. The petulant tone rose again to yell "I said I didn't want to come in the first place!" A red faced and embarrassed Prince Charles pretended not to hear his bride as he checked his double-barrelled shotgun, seemingly oblivious to the zero temperatures and the icy rain.

Muffled against the January weather in a windcheater and woolly hat Princess Diana had made the mistake of going on a pheasant shoot because her husband had asked her to accompany him. The Princess has never much liked Charles' endless sporting activities. She had watched him on polo field at Windsor with enjoyment. From the deck of the Royal Yacht Britannia she had admired his skill on a wind surfing board. She had gone to foxhunts with him and sat patiently in her car while he galloped off across the muddy fields. She had even let him teach her to fish for salmon, and stood thigh-high in icy water just to be by his side.

BUT ON this cold day, when Princess Diana lost her temper, any husband should have known better than to insist that his wife join in his sport. Trudging across a muddy field as her husband shot down game birds was not her idea of fun.

She kept up her tirade against Charles until the Prince could take it no longer. He got into his estate car and drove off, leaving her behind with the rest of the Royal shooting party, which included Prince Philip and Princess Anne's husband Captain Mark Phillips. They pretended not to notice. It was a lovers' quarrel, a further demonstration that Charles and his young bride were just like other newly weds. They were facing a situation as old as Adam and Eve – the problem of settling down together.

Learning to live with each other was not so easy for the Royal lovers. They were (and still are) surrounded by servants, policemen and Palace officials. Almost every minute of each day seems to be governed by strict protocol. It is difficult to close the door of an apartment and have a private row like most young marrieds.

Prince Charles is inclined to be very selfish in his pursuit of what he considers to be pleasure and Diana had, on this occasion in January, decided to put her foot down in public. This was a new side of the Princess, never seen before, totally alien from the view the world then had of Diana, peeking shyly out from under her blonde fringe with very little to say for herself.

The responsibility of marriage did not come easily to Charles. The problems for Diana and the stories about her health and her temper began again soon after the birth of Prince William. One famous British gossip writer even went so far to describe the Princess of Wales as a "monster." Charles was pictured as a wimp with a diamond hard wife.

Diana herself did not help at that time. She and Charles had obviously been rowing when he turned up, alone, for the November Remembrance Day service after William's birth. Staff were hurriedly told that the Princess would not be joining him for this important public engagement. But minutes later Diana turned up, driving her own car, and very late. She went into the Royal Albert Hall through a side door. Palace officials blamed an administrative error for the late arrival for such a solemn ceremony, an excuse which was never believed for a moment.

EVENTUALLY the stories and the gossip about the Princess mounted, not helped by the sudden departures of a number of Prince Charles' former staff and friends during his bachelor years. The Queen intervened over worries of the stress and pressure on Diana and what she described as "grossly exaggerated reports." She asked Fleet Street editors to leave Diana alone, hinting that if the stories went on Diana could suffer a breakdown.

The problems were not helped by the fact that the young Princess insisted on reading every word written about her in the gossip columns, something other members of the family would never dream of doing. For them, these sometimes incredible fantasies are just the subject of dinner table jokes. But for the then immature Princess it was taken very seriously. She even went out and bought copies of women's magazines which built her up to be some sort of superstar with fabulous beauty, and she felt she had to live up to that unobtainable image. It was altogether too much for such a young girl.

Charles and Diana overcame this difficult period in their marriage because of their genuine and deep love for each other. You only have to be in the same room to sense their mutual affection. They do a lot of touching and hand holding. (He even slyly pinches her bottom in public whenever he gets the chance, especially when they stand side by side for official photographs. His hand begins to wander and still smiling, out of sight of the cameramen, she slaps it back).

THEIRS is no arranged marriage of convenience to secure the dynasty of the House of Windsor. The marriage of the Prince and Princess of Wales is based on the warmth of their family love. The ironic sense of humour and the laughter they share pulled them through Diana's difficult time of adjusting to her public pedestal. There is a theory that Charles, once almost a confirmed bachelor and very set in his ways, fell deeper in love with his wife as their marriage matured.

They have their ups and downs, just like any other married couple. And Charles is prepared to admit, although Diana won't (in public anyway) that they do have the occasional fight. But not many people have to live up to the expectations of a world which wants a fairy tale story of a Royal marriage made in heaven.

She now knows the price she had to pay for being Princess of Wales is a lifetime of polite conversation. Diana has learnt never to appear anything other than beautiful, radiant and gracious in public. The first two years, at times, were not easy for either of them. Even now they have to fight back at the gossips who try to hack away at their marriage. But love and the joy over two perfect children has turned them into a sound partnership. They now laugh at their tiffs, even their public ones.

When Diana stalked off in a huff after what was

later described as a "misunderstanding" skiing in the Swiss Alps, the Prince just said wryly "I'll get it in the neck now."

Perhaps one clue to the strength of their marriage comes from Diana's own childhood. The young Diana was what would now be called a tug-of-love child. She was pulled backwards and forwards between her mother and father and, in between, sent to boarding schools.

The rift in the Spencer household was far from amicable. Her mother, Frances, was only 18 when she walked up the aisle of Westminster Abbey in 1954, a society event which was hailed as the wedding of the year. The marriage floundered an unlucky 13 years later, and after bearing four children (Diana was then just six years old). Frances decided, at the age of 31, to make a completely new life for herself. She walked out of the family home creating a huge social scandal at the time. Diana knew little of the bitterness of the acrimonious divorce that followed in 1969.

Diana's father, then Lord Althorp, denied his wife's allegations of marital cruelty and filed for divorce on the grounds of his wife's adultery with Mr Shand Kydd (who Frances later married) at an hotel near Kensington Palace. This was shockingly "bad form" in aristocratic circles.

The problem was that Frances, a headstrong lady with Irish blood, had not really had time to live, to see much of life, before her marriage to a much older man.

Diana was both homesick and naughty at Riddlesworth Hall, a preparatory school near Diss in Norfolk. The enormous amount of love she had before she was six must have made life very lonely for her. Childhood friends and her father's household staff never described the future Princess of Wales as a shy girl. Lots of confidence, were the words they used. "Shy" was a newspaper term.

Of all the millions of words written on the former Lady Diana Spencer since the announcement of her engagement she has only ever really objected to one description – sweet. Her dislike of being called "sweet" may account for the threads of steel that occasionally creep into that well-scrubbed but not over plummy voice.

Princess Diana doesn't mind shy, innocent, modest or even quiet...but "sweet" – that was going too far, "I'm a normal person" said the future Queen of England, "And I love life." In the first five years of marriage members of the Royal household and even the future King were to feel that steel.

THE LIFE HE LEFT BEHIND

ON FEBRUARY 24 1981, as Prince Charles was showing his future bride to the world's Press in the back garden of Buckingham Palace, the band of the Coldstream Guards marched to the front playing *"Now Your Philandering Days Are Over."* This song from the Marriage of Figaro seemed very appropriate because Prince Charles must have known this was the end of an exciting era. So did Diana. According to her friends she made it plain to Charles before accepting his proposal that his long history of risking his neck and his adventurous bachelor life were going to have to change. From the day of the engagement she no longer called him "Sir" but "Darling," – (in public, and to others, she always refers to "My husband") and she laid down a few ground rules of her own. She knew that a man who had enjoyed his pick of almost every beauty was going to be difficult to live with. Then there was the question of a discreet house in London where he used to meet his friends privately, and the two married women who had been so close to the Heir to the Throne in the five years before his engagement.

Apart from his former ladies, the future Princess was worried about her husband-to-be's desire to prove what a macho man he was by constantly dicing with death. His penchant for danger also worried the Queen, so Diana had a strong ally at the Palace. He had the habit of jumping head first into any activity that got the Royal adrenalin flowing. As a pilot in the Navy and the RAF he flew every type of aircraft, from Commando helicopters to 1,000 miles an hour Phantom jets. His first parachute jump during his RAF training nearly ended in disaster when he found himself descending towards the sea upside down with his legs caught in the rigging lines. Despite this, when he was made Colonel-in-Chief of the Parachute Regiment he decided to carry out a full training programme with the other paras to earn his wings – and again on one jump he succeeded in getting his lines twisted.

He had even dived under the Arctic ice and, as the skipper of a warship, hunted for Russian submarines. He lavished £50,000 a year (and still does) on a stable of polo ponies, his greatest extravagance. He has been thrown badly on at least four occasions and been kicked more than once, including a severe blow to the head.

He once had a hoof-shaped bruise near his heart, and still carries the scar on his cheek from a clash on the polo field which needed nine stitches. His favourite steeplechaser, Allibar, worth £15,000 died from a heart attack while he was riding him. Little wonder that the Queen had been pleading with her eldest son to start taking things a little easier. Why did he risk his neck so often? According to Charles it was a matter of: "I always like pushing myself to the limit, just to see how far I can go. I get terrified at times."

In the last five years Diana hasn't had all that much success persuading her husband to give up his dangerous sports. He still plays polo, but not quite so vigorously as before, and he still goes hunting, urging his mount on over steep hedges and into dense woodland. Fatal hunting accidents are not unknown, and Diana must worry sometimes as he sets out early in the mornings to chase a fox. But Charles' string of polo ponies could never match his string of ex-girl friends. Diana had always known about his reputation as a ladies man. After all, even her own sister Lady Sarah was one of the Charlie set, or "Charlie's Angels" as some people called them.

Prince Charles' girls ranged from his first love at Cambridge University when he was only 18, from the stunning dark-haired and fiery Chilean Lucia Santa Cruz, to the sexy blonde British actress Susan George. Over the years the sailor Prince had left girls in many ports and most of them remained friends, keeping happy memories of their relationships, even after they went off and married other men. They were usually fair and sexy, and many said after they were dropped for yet another new face "Charles was very romantic, he always made you feel that you are the only woman in the world – for a while anyway."

Throughout his many years of discreet meetings in the country, or quietly at his Buckingham Palace apartments, Prince Charles had the pick of the best, but he only really fell in love twice before proposing to Diana. Just before the engagement he sold a £100,000 hideaway house he had kept two miles from the Palace, a house to which Diana was once invited for a quiet, candle-lit dinner. The nearest pub is called, appropriately enough, the Windsor Castle, but despite this no one ever discovered his hideaway or other secret trysting places. Charles would often speed off in his 140 mph Aston Martin sports car to cottages tucked away in different parts of the country.

BUT IT could easily have been Princess Anna or Princess Davina rather than Diana, for although Prince Charles had a reputation as a ladies' man, he was not only shy but very old-fashioned in his approach to women. He became briefly infatuated with many beauties but fell in love seriously with only three. Naturally enough, for a man in this enviable position, as one of the world's most eligible bachelors, he seemed for the main part to be happy with being single. His relationships were arranged with enormous discretion, and apart from a few brief flings with actresses, he stuck to his own kind; wealthy, socially acceptable young ladies who could be relied upon not to talk, especially to the Press, about their friendship with the future King.

He began every relationship with flowers, large bouquets of red roses, and then always the same system, the telephone call and the suggestion of a quiet supper, or perhaps, as he got to know the lady better, a weekend in the country staying with reliable and non-talkative friends. He liked to do the running and was put out if a girl had the audacity to ring him even if he had given her his private number. There must have been a lot of ladies who cried into their handkerchieves waiting for the elusive Royal call that never came.

There was little opportunity for the Prince to be alone with a girl. His apartments at Buckingham Palace, a simple sitting room and bedroom overlooking St. James' Park, were unsuitable for any secret liaison, but he did manage to sneak quite a few up to his rooms for supper, including the stunning and very sexy blonde actress, Susan George, whom he first met at a film premiere in 1978.

He was only ever seen with her once in public, at his 30th birthday party when she was just one of hundreds of guests, but they met often and discreetly, for dinner either in the Palace or at Windsor Castle. The relationship between the Prince and the showgirl could never have worked, but they enjoyed each other's company and loyally Miss George has never once tried to gain publicity by speaking of her Royal friendship.

Other girls came and went, but no one ever seemed to spend the night at the Palace. His ex-valet, Stephen Barry, unsportingly revealed this after he left the Prince's employ, saying "in all those twelve years that I worked for him if he was meant to be in his bed in the morning when I went to wake him up, he was in bed, alone."

There were precious few Princesses in ivory towers waiting for Prince Charles to fly in on his helicopter and whisk them away. Charles was never interested in any of the daughters of the rest of the European Royals. A tentative move was made by the late Princess Grace of Monaco to introduce her raven haired daughter, Princess Caroline, to Charles, but she was too dark and sultry and not his type at all...for this very English gentleman really did prefer blondes, especially those with curves in the right places.

Beauties who drifted in and out of his life from the time he left university to his meeting with Lady Diana Spencer, were mostly cool blondes. Charles fell in and out of love easily. He was quickly infatuated by a beautiful face but soon tired. There was a long list of girls in his life, but apart from Diana, the Prince only considered actually marrying two. The first real love affair was ruined by details of the lady's past romances being made public, and the other by the conditions of secrecy under which the Royal love affair was conducted.

Davina Sheffield was the first, and she would have made a superb Princess of Wales, tall and blonde with a stunning smile. Very similar in fact to Princess Diana, but more mature. The Prince treated Davina, whom he met in 1974, much more openly than any of his other girlfriends, and there was little of the secrecy which had always surrounded his previous affairs. She lunched with the Queen and went to Balmoral for the summer holidays. She stayed the course, and passed all the tests: the Prince always wanted to make sure that his girls understood that holidays in the Scottish countryside are only for the hardy and not those wanting to dance the night away.

His idea of a perfect day out was spending hours up to his thighs in the chilling waters of the River Dee casting for salmon. Many of the girls who went to Scotland were also required to freeze on the Norfolk fields as the Prince shot pheasants. Those who could not stand the course were struck off the Prince's address book. One, Georgina Russell, the beautiful daughter of British Ambassador, Sir John Russell, hated the cold and told the Prince quite plainly "I'm bored." He laughed about it afterwards with his staff and she went home from what she later called "a beastly holiday" and never saw Charles

again. Davina was different. She loved the countryside, the hunting, shooting and fishing, and they were obviously in love. The romance went on for nearly two years, but their affair was shattered by some unpleasant revelations from the past. An ex-lover, one James Beard, told the story of his romance with the Prince's girl in a Sunday newspaper and how he had lived with her for six months in an Eleventh Century cottage with roses round the door.

That ruined Davina's chances...she went to Saigon to look after orphaned children, and when she returned she saw the Prince occasionally, but all hope of marriage had gone. The Prince of Wales could not wed anyone who had been involved in anything that even smacked of a scandal, no matter what his own personal feelings might have been. A pity, for Davina, once described by a British tabloid newspaper as a "big, blonde bombshell" had exactly the right breeding and style for the job as Princess of Wales; upper class and a cousin of a member of the House of Lords, Lord McGowan.

At one time Charles was so keen on Davina that he even put a bikini clad photograph of her in his cabin when he served on HMS Bronington. Family tree experts even discovered that she and Charles were distantly related, 18th cousins, twice removed.

After it was all over it didn't take Davina long to find a husband. She married Old Etonian Jonathan Morley, ten years older than her and a divorcé. She's now 34 and has a two-year-old son.

THE Prince was out hunting when he met the second big love of his life. Sitting on his horse, waiting for the Belvoir Hunt to move off across muddy Leicestershire fields in the autumn of 1979, he spotted a beautiful blonde on horseback. He asked for her telephone number and began the usual English gentleman approach, flowers to the door of her flat and an invitation to dinner.

The lady on the horse was a truly marvellous-looking woman, tall blonde and curvy, with a sparkling personality and tremendous presence. Anna Wallace, then 25 years old and the daughter of a Scottish landowner, became Prince Charles' constant companion through the winter of 1979 to 1980. They spent many weekends together at the homes of friends in the country and he made many nightly visits to her flat near Harrods, just off Sloane Street.

Anna was introduced to the Queen, and stayed the cold course at Balmoral. She seemed perfect for the role as Princess of Wales, discreet and intelligent, and the couple were very much in love. Unfortunately, Miss Wallace was a substantial person in her own right who had earned the nickname of "whiplash" over her passionate, hot temper. She hated all the secrecy which surrounded their romance, the furtive meetings, mostly arranged through the Royal detectives, the hurried departures after weekends in the country and, most of all, the fact that she was rarely allowed to be seen in public with her man.

IN THE spring of 1980, the Prince of Wales, deeply in love with Anna, is said to have proposed marriage to her. Anna wanted time to think, but unfortunately during this thinking period her headstrong temper came to the fore and ruined her chances. The Prince and his love rowed in public at the Queen Mother's eightieth birthday party. Quite simply Anna did not feel that her lover was giving her enough attention. The more he acted the part of the gentleman and danced with the other ladies present, the angrier she got. Eventually she walked out on him, declaring loudly "I've never been treated so badly in all my life." The Prince didn't give up, he sent his detective round to her flat with a message of forgiveness, but fiery Anna ignored his pleas.

Just a few weeks later she announced her engagement in *The Times*, right next to the court circular where Prince Charles could not fail to see it. Within a few months of the break-up of this affair, Anna had married Johnny Hesketh, the younger brother of Lord Hesketh. Charles was deeply hurt and some Royal insiders felt that he married Lady Diana Spencer on the rebound.

There was no real happiness for Anna. Her marriage to Johnny Hesketh didn't last, and the couple separated after only a few months. Wealthy (she has two homes, one in Chelsea the other in the Belvoir country where she hunts) amusing and attractive Anna is now a well known face on the London party and social scene, and is always refered to in the gossip columns as "Prince Charles' ex." It is a label she will wear for the rest of her life.

Another who flitted briefly through Charles' life was Lady Sarah Spencer, his wife's older sister. Charles took pretty, red-haired Sarah, a lively and vivacious girl, with him to Klosters in Switzerland for a skiing holiday. They stayed at a tiny two-bedroomed chalet with another couple, and the place was so cramped that the Prince's detective had to sleep on the floor beside the front door. At that time Diana was still at school with a photograph of Prince Charles above her bed. There was said never to have been a big romance between Sarah and Charles, just friendship, and their close relationship ended abruptly after Sarah unwisely announced to a reporter that she was not in love with the Prince of Wales.

Another girl strongly tipped for the job as Princess of Wales also failed to stay the course, but it wasn't the freezing moors of Scotland which sent her packing. Lady Jane Wellesley, the daughter of the Duke of Wellington, small, dark and beautiful, wasn't really Charles' type, but strangely enough they got on enormously well as friends, though nothing more. She hated the Pressmen who followed her everywhere. She wanted peace and quiet, something a future Princess of Wales could never have.

☆ ☆ ☆ ☆ ☆

BORN TO BE KING

PREPARING FOR HIS ROLE IN LIFE

THE BRIDEGROOM'S formal title is His Royal Highness the Prince Charles Philip Arthur George, Prince of Wales and Earl of Chester, Duke of Cornwall and Rothesay, Earl of Carrick and Baron of Renfrew, Lord of the Isles and Great Steward of Scotland, Knight of The Garter. The Prince of Wales and Earl of Chester are joint titles most closely associated with a male Heir Apparent of a reigning Monarch. They go back to Edward II who had them conferred on him in February 1301. On the death of a Prince of Wales and Earl of Chester in the lifetime of a Sovereign the titles do not pass on to the current holder's son. They must be recreated with each reign.

Cornwall and the five Scottish titles came, by tradition, to Charles as eldest son of the Sovereign, from the moment the Queen ascended to the Throne. Edward III created his son Duke of Cornwall in March 1337 making it clear that the title should descend to the eldest son of the Kings and Queens of England forever. The Scottish titles go back to the Seventeenth Century. They were brought to England when

James the Sixth of Scotland became James the First of England after the death of the first Queen Elizabeth. Charles is now the holder of them as Heir to the old kingdom of Scotland.

He was born at Buckingham Palace on the evening of 14 November, 1948, the first male in direct succession for more than eighty years. His ancestors include such unlikely figures as the first president of the United States, George Washington, and the Prophet of Islam, Mohammed. As Prince of Wales he is in the ancestral line of a pageant of Royalty that includes Edward, the classical armour-clad Black Prince of the Fourteenth Century – who used to feature in so many Hollywood epics starring either Robert Taylor or Tony Curtis – the marriage-prone Henry VIII, and the man who gave his name to both a style of living and an era, Queen Victoria's son, Edward VII. Discovery of his fate came to Charles when he was about eight-years-old, "in the most ghastly, inexorable sense." He remembers: "I didn't suddenly wake up in my pram one day and say 'Yippee.' I think it just dawns on you slowly, that people are interested in you and you slowly get the idea that you have a certain duty and responsibility. I think it's better that way, rather than someone suddenly telling you." He knows he will one day represent an institution constantly under attack, and that he will be King of a country that has known better days. He has a great faith in Britain, however, and a strong belief, in what the country still stands for.

In childhood Charles was somewhat shy and introverted, in contrast to Anne, who was ebullient and outward going. As a toddler he would snuggle up beside his mother on a settee and look quietly at a picture book, or listen to her as she read him a story. The most popular ones were the *Tales of Beatrix Potter* and the adventures of *Baba the Elephant* and *Tin-Tin*. He had enough boyish spirit in him, however, for the Queen, just like any other mother, to have to cope with the pranks and mischief of her son. He raced round the corridors of Buckingham Palace with his friends, played risky games of hide-and-seek on the roof of Windsor Castle, or slipped pieces of ice down the collar of a footman. When he deserved it he would get a good spanking, particularly if he was caught being rude to the servants. The Queen took a very stern view of this. Her Majesty also taught him the value of money, restricting his pocket money to the equivalent of twelve pence a week until he was ten-years-old, when he was given a rise which made it twenty-five pence. As part of the training for a ceremonial life, Charles and Anne were taught to stand motionless for long periods, to accustom them to the duties ahead.

Hundreds of requests came for the young Prince to make public appearances but the Queen resisted them all, no matter how worthy the cause. She remembered how, as a young Princess in the war years, she was suddenly thrust into the public arena and she insisted that her son should first of all have a normal childhood, as far as this could be arranged. So the Queen protected Charles and brought him up carefully to the stage when he was gradually made aware of his state duties. Her Majesty was also determined that her son would not become a Palace wastrel, a mere understudy, deprived of any responsibility and forever waiting in the wings. She had seen too much of this in the history of her family. Charles was to be made aware of his future role at the right time, and be prepared for it.

The Queen took special care over the education of the Prince. Sending Charles away to school, rather than having the traditional private tuition for him, was to set a Royal precedent. She decided that, unlike his predecessors, he should go out and meet his future subjects. Her Majesty had been educated behind the railings of Buckingham Palace by a succession of governes-

ses and tutors. Charles was given the chance to go beyond the Royal stockade, and live among ordinary people. She helped her son through all the usual growing pains of youth and his moments of bewilderment at life. Her encouragement was always there whenever he thought the going was too tough. When he first went away to school she wrote to him almost daily, feeding him family gossip to keep up his spirits. At university Charles occasionally found the task a struggle and felt lonely. The Queen would visit him privately in his rooms at Trinity College, where they would talk over his problems while he fried a simple meal for the two of them.

The Queen attended to her son's upbringing with a typical mother's gentleness but Prince Philip provided a grittier influence. Royal paternal attitudes have changed considerably since the beginning of his century. Charles and Philip have a very close relationship, based not on fear, but on love and respect for each other's achievements. Their personalities differ considerably. Prince Philip has always been the more abrasive while Charles has more gentleness of spirit. One of the Duke's friends once said: "Charles is not a bit like him."

At first Charles seemed to try hard to emulate his father. He was tempted to adopt Philip's occasional high-handed style. But as he grew out of his teens the Prince developed a likeable personality of his own, while his father began to mellow. They tend to have the same mannerisms: the brisk walk, the habit of clenching their hands behind their backs, and tossing their heads when laughing; Charles, too, walks around with his left hand thrust casually into his jacket pocket. He has inherited his father's sense of humour; both like zany, outrageous slapstick rather than sharpness of wit.

Otherwise their tastes are usually quite different. Charles adores music for instance, whereas Prince Philip often finds it a trial to have to sit through a concert. The young Prince can enjoy solitary pastimes, while the Duke is much more gregarious. Some people close to the family think Princess Anne, Prince Andrew and Prince Edward take more after their father than the eldest son. When Charles was a child, Prince Philip was determined that his son would not have a pampered life. When Charles was a schoolboy, Philip once noticed a servant hurrying to close a door that his son had failed to shut. He shouted: "Leave it alone. He's got hands. He can go back and do it himself."

Like the Queen, Prince Philip wanted him to rub up against other children, and to see how others lived. He said: "We want him to go to school with other boys of his generation and to learn to live with other children. To absorb from his childhood the discipline imposed by education with others." He also wanted Charles to pick up a few bruises and get used to the hard knocks of tough physical activities. Dancing lessons were stopped, music lessons cut down and, instead, Charles was sent off to a playing field in Chelsea to get into the rough and tumble of soccer with other youngsters. He also went to a private gymnasium twice a week for gymnastic work-outs.

Prince Philip took him out in bitter wintry weather to teach him to shoot in the mud and puddles of marshes and over the heather around Balmoral, where Charles shot his first grouse when he was ten-years-old. He taught him how to fish as well.

When Philip was at home he would spend an hour after tea teaching his son to swim in the pool at Buckingham Palace. Charles took to the water without a hint of nervousness and could swim a length before he was five-years-old. Father and son would have a boisterous game of football in the Palace grounds, with the corgis barking round their heels. Now and again the Queen and toddler Anne might join in the fun.

Nearly all his physical skills were taught to Charles by his father. In this way they grew closer to each other and Philip was delighted to see his son developing into a self-confident youngster. But Charles has never had the Duke's ambition to excel at organised games. He still shows little enthusiasm for team games, such as rugby, soccer and cricket. Individual achievement, where he is testing himself rather than others, has been his forte, hence the generally solitary pursuits he tends to go in for...diving, surfing, flying. His only concession to 'team spirit' is polo.

Philip introduced his son to sailing, but Charles did not develop the same passion for it as his father, and the two rarely go sailing together these days because they do not seem to see eye-to-eye when they are in a boat. Charles explains frankly: "I remember one disastrous day when we were racing and my father was shouting instructions. We wound the winch harder and the sail split in half with a sickening crack. Father was not pleased. Not long after that I was banned from the boat after an incident cruising off Scotland. There was no wind and I was amusing myself taking pot-shots at beer cans floating around the boat. The only gust of the day blew the jib in front of my rifle just as I fired. I wasn't invited back on board." The Duke in consultation with the Queen and her advisers, also influenced the choice of schools for their offspring.

He had his way first over the preparatory school Charles went to before moving on to public school. Philip attended Cheam School, which is set in sixty-five acres of grounds on the Berkshire border. It has a history of teaching the aristocracy and the sons of the rich going back as far as the early Seventeenth Century. Charles, too was sent there.

The really decisive part played by the Royal father in helping to bring out the manly qualities in Charles was when the time came to select a senior school for him. Eton, the traditional establishment for top young English gentlemen, was, at first, favoured by the Queen. Charles' name had been put down for a place when he was born. Philip had other ideas. He wanted – and got – his own *alma mater*: tough, authoritarian Gordonstoun set in a bleak stretch of Northern Scotland in Morayshire and based on the principles of the German educationalist Dr. Kurt Hahn. Gordonstoun had been good enough for the Duke. He thought its harsh, cold-shower regime had done him a world of good, so why should it not do the same for his eldest son?

When the young Prince went there he was still fairly shy and withdrawn. Charles remembers now that all the tales he had heard about it made the school seem "pretty gruesome." It was a very nervous young man who was flown by his father up to Morayshire to start his few bracing years there. Philip reminded him "not to let the side down."

The place was mainly a collection of crude huts. Charles' dormitory had unpainted wooden walls, bare floors and uncomfortable iron beds. There was the obligatory cold shower to be taken every morning, no matter what the weather. As the school is situated in one of the more exposed and rugged parts of Scotland, the temperature was usually at shivering level. Even the school motto – *'Plus est en vous'* (There is more in you) – typified a harsh system aimed at stretching to the full both physical and intellectual capabilities.

To bring him down to earth and away from any fancy ideas he might have of being a special sort of fellow from the land of palaces, his housemaster gave Charles a particularly humiliating daily task in his first term – emptying the dustbins. Charles may have been reluctant to be submitted to the rigours of Gordonstoun, but he never quarrelled with his father's decision.

He disliked the school at first, became terribly homesick and did not fit easily into the regime. After four years Charles ended up loving the place, just as his father had done. He became head boy and, shrugging his shoulders, pointed out that it was not really as tough as he had expected it to be. He excelled in geography and modern languages, captained the school's cricket and hockey teams and represented Gordonstoun in inter-school athletics meetings. He also took the title role in a production of 'Macbeth.'

Charles has a fascination for history which he carried with him from Gordonstoun to Trinity College, Cambridge, where he studied archaeology and anthropology during his first year. He had an average Class II Division I pass in his tripos on these subjects before switching to modern history for his last two years at university, and the end of which he took a Bachelor of Arts Honours degree. "When you meet as many people as I do, you become curious about what makes men tick and what makes men tick differently."

His exam papers are preserved for posterity in the Royal library at Windsor. His tutor on social anthropology commented in a supervision report: "He writes useful and thoughtful essays. although sometimes they are a little rushed. He is interested in discussion – likes to draw parallels between the peoples we study and ourselves."

At Cambridge he also developed a love for the stage and knock-about farce. He appeared in undergraduate revues, and earned himself the nickname 'Clown Prince.' He has links with Australia that go back to his schooldays, when he spent a year at Timbertops – the abrasive, open-air school on the mountains north of Melbourne. He has returned to Australia regularly ever since.

With his love of risking his neck now and again, he goes down well with a people who like a man to prove his courage. He regards the year he spent at school in Australia as "the most wonderful period" in his life. The Australians responded to his affection for their country and themselves with such endearing terms as "Good on yer, Pommy bastard." Part of his transition from nervous teenager to confident man took place there; away from the protecting arms of his family he learned to stand alone.

The Prince's liking for swimming fits in perfectly with Australia's beach-side way of life. When he paid an official visit in 1974 he spent as much time as possible in the sometimes treacherous, rolling seas. At Coolangatta he watched local beach rescue squads in operation in the risky surf. He persuaded the beach guards and anxious local officials to allow him to ride in a powerful new rescue craft. Once in the boat he took over the controls himself, and flew across the waves.

During that tour of Australia and New Zealand he rolled up his sleeves and joined the sheep shearers. These men, who earn their living clipping wool to clothe people throughout the world, are among the toughest and roughest workers anywhere. Charles took to them immediately, and they to him, when he called at a sheep station near Wellington, New Zealand.

Their way of life interested him. He asked them about their homes, their families, and what they wanted in the future. Then the 'gaffer' of the shearers asked Charles to lend a hand. A dozen or so bewildered beasts were brought up and

H.R.H. swung into action with a pole, pushing the sheep through a murky, foul-smelling dip. It was a bit of a struggle and he doubted whether he could ever have earned a week's wages on the job. But he learned a little more about one tiny part of his future domaine.

The Queen made Charles a Knight of The Garter, one of the oldest orders of chivalry in the world, when he was ten-years-old, but he was not invested and installed in the Royal Chapel at Windsor until 1968, when he reached the age of twenty. One of his first formal steps towards the eventual responsibility of the Throne was in the autumn of 1972 when, at the age of twenty-three, he was appointed a Councillor of State – together with the Queen Mother – to handle the official affairs of the realm while the Queen visited Australia.

This function is vital to the running of Britain and the Commonwealth because, constitutionally, the works of governments at home and abroad have to be officially approved by the Sovereign or her properly appointed representatives.

Charles' interest in the social conditions of modern life, his awareness of community problems, and concern for the well-being of the nation have been demonstrated in his work for Wales. When the Queen and Prince Philip decided the time had come for Charles to take up the title of Prince of Wales, they were determined that, unlike the late Duke of Windsor when he bore the same name, their son was to develop more than just a nodding acquaintance with the place. He was to learn the Welsh language and culture and the history of the Principality.

His involvement in all things Welsh now includes being Colonel-in-Chief of the Welsh Guards, the youngest regiment of the Brigade of Guards. It is in their uniform that he rides with his mother every June to take part in the most spectacular ceremony of Trooping the Colour, on Horse Guards Parade in London. He first donned the white-plumed bearskin and scarlet jacket for this celebration of the Sovereign's Official Birthday while he was in the Royal Navy in 1975. Since then, and for the future, it has become one of the most important yearly engagements in his diary.

This mounting involvement in public events has taken the Heir closer to millions on a global scale. He feels nothing is too much trouble if it helps to establish a link with those he will rule.

BORN
TO BE QUEEN

GROWING UP WITH THE ROYAL CHILDREN

THE FUTURE Queen of England was born in the middle of the hottest afternoon for years. She was a perfectly formed, healthy bouncing seven pound baby and her parents, Frances and Johnny, were both delighted of course with the latest addition to their family. They already had two daughters and they had lost a baby son tragically.

They had hoped and prayed for another son, a future heir for the considerable family fortune, and on this afternoon, the first day of July 1961 they had not thought of one single girl's name in expectation of a boy. But the new baby took her first public engagement calmly and without tears as she was christened Diana Frances Spencer in a Norfolk parish church. As if in anticipation of her destiny in just nineteen years, she was born on land and property owned by the British Royal Family. The large country home, Park House, was just a stone's throw from Sandringham.

With an illustrious lineage which stretched all the way back to the rule of Charles II, Diana was born, like her older sisters Jane and Sarah, with an automatic title. Diana's family were distantly related to the Royal Family, and her father, Edward, the eighth Earl Spencer, known as "Johnny" to his family, was very close friends with the Queen and Prince Philip. He was also an equerry to the Queen. Living on the Sandringham estate, Diana virtually grew up with the Royal children.

There was just a low dry stone wall to separate their homes and the three Princes and their Princess sister would regularly climb over to share the small open air swimming pool at Park House. Her regular playmate was Prince Andrew, an angelic looking boy two years older than herself. Looking back now, Diana cannot remember meeting the much older, and to her as a little girl somewhat mysterious, Prince Charles. As Diana grew up at Park House, Charles was away at preparatory or boarding school. He must have first seen her when she was still in nappies and he was a thirteen or fourteen-year-old schoolboy heading rapidly for manhood.

Neither Charles nor Diana can really remember meeting before November 1977, the year of the Queen's Silver Jubilee. The Spencers, their family split by the trauma of divorce, had by then moved to their ancestral home, Althorp in Northamptonshire. It was Diana's older sister Sarah, who introduced the two as they stood in a muddy ploughed field. Charles had come to Althorp for a day's hunting and he recalled later thinking at the time "what a very jolly, amusing and attractive sixteen-year-old." Although he would meet her on a number of other occasions it would be three years before the courtship really began.

Diana is remembered as a toddler who grew up to be a trouble free, happy child. Her first governess, Gertrude Allen, now in her seventies, patiently and dutifully read and listened to the infant Diana in the nursery at Park House. "A very conscientious child, she would always try," recalled Miss Allen. That is how everyone remembers the little girl with the bright blue eyes and the sort of English peaches-and-cream complexion that ladies of other nations would murder for.

Diana was always thoughtful, the sort of little girl who was always the first to put a log on the fire, a practical girl who would go round Park House in winter closing the shutters. Diana remembers her childhood at Park House as "a good time of my life." She was too young to remember the unhappiness and heartbreak which split the Spencer family in 1967.

The divorce meant that the four Spencer children saw their mother only rarely, but they all adored their father who had won the court case for their custody. But as Diana grew, so did the emotional links between mother and daughter. Frances' influence was to grow stronger in Diana's adolescent years. Her father lived a solitary life until 1976 when he married Raine, Countess of Dartmouth, the daughter of best-selling romantic novelist Barbara Cartland. The little girl moved on to school, first at Riddlesworth Hall, a private preparatory school in Diss, Norfolk, not far from Park House, and then to West Heath, a boarding school in Kent. During her holidays she played with the young Royal set from next door and became used to meeting the Queen and Prince Philip in a way that meant she was never in awe of them. To Diana it was rather like meeting one's father's bosses, and her relaxed attitude in their company would pave the way for the romance of 1980.

At West Heath, and later at a Swiss finishing school, Diana received a typical British middle-class education, but not an intellectual one. Her school friends remember her as a fun-loving, easy-going and considerate girl, the kind of person who never forgot to send birthday cards on the right day. Her interests were looking after young children, swimming, classical music, ballet and later skiing.

A typical school report for the West Heath academy where Diana studied between 1973 and 1977 would have revealed that she had average marks in English, but showed a keen interest in history – understandably with her family background. She had a natural talent for art lessons and was an excellent pupil in the dance classes. Just a few months before her courtship started in earnest Diana tried to teach Charles how to tap dance on a concrete terrace at Sandringham; her lesson ended with them both roaring with laughter. At school she slept with a picture of Prince Charles above her bed.

The placing of the photograph was a very strange coincidence, specially in view of the way things turned out. The photograph, of the Prince's Investiture as Prince of Wales in 1969, was presented to the school by former newspaper chief Cecil King, whose grand-daughter was a pupil. The picture became a favourite with Diana and the girls who shared her plain white-painted dormitory. The photograph is still hanging in the room to this day.

Headmistress, Miss Ruth Rudge, remembers that Diana was a delight to have at the school. She was so popular that on her leaving day she was presented with a cup for special services to the school. "She was always helpful and willing," recalled Miss Rudge. "The dining room staff liked her a lot because she used to help them with laying tables and clearing up."

Life at school was quite spartan. At 7.30 a.m. sharp the rising bell would ring. Lessons continued until 7.00 p.m. with an extra session on saturday morning. Lady Diana remembers West Heath as "a thoroughly enjoyable time." While she was still at school her father and her sisters had left the ten-bedroomed Park House for much bigger surroundings at Althorp.

In 1975 Edward Spencer inherited the family seat from his father, Jack, becoming the Eighth Earl. The Sixteenth Century stately house at Althorp is one of Britain's best kept houses and it contains the cream of the contents of five homes once owned by the Spencer family. The house is filled with pictures by Rubens, Poussin, Van Dyck, Gainsborough, Reynolds and many others. There is also some fine furniture and extensive collections of porcelain and silver. For Diana, her two elder sisters and her younger brother Charles, it was like moving into a museum. Diana was sharing her holidays between Althorp and her mother's new home on the Scottish Island of Seil where her new stepfather ran a beef farm.

Her relationship with her mother was growing closer and closer.

It was during this time of getting used to living in Althorp and flitting between Northampton-shire, her school in Kent and her mother in

Scotland, that her future stepmother entered her life. Raine Dartmouth's arrival at Althorp sparked off quite a stir among the Spencer children. Raine was like a heroine from one of her mother's, Barbara Cartland's, novels.

At the age of eighteen she had been married to a handsome Guards officer, Gerald Legge, who later became the Earl of Dartmouth. Lady Diana's father was at Eton with him. A slim health fanatic with a porcelain complexion, Raine had boundless energy. At the age of twenty-three she became Westminster's youngest councillor and was famous all over Britain for her welfare work. In 1976, the year after Edward became Earl Spencer, Raine parted from the man she used to describe as "so steady and strong" and moved into Althorp to be with her husband's old school friend.

The Earl of Dartmouth cited Lady Diana's father in the divorce action which followed, but the judge granted a decree because of Raine's "adultery with a man against whom the charge has not been proved." Two months after the divorce Raine became Countess Spencer. All four Spencer children, including Diana, stayed away from the ceremony which was a very small affair with only two witnesses. Even Raine's mother, Barbara Cartland wasn't invited. Her daughter just rang her after the ceremony to say "Hello, we're married."

Diana saw little of her stepmother, but Lady Sarah made her feelings very clear by telling a gossip writer, "Lady Dartmouth is an all-too frequent visitor." Raine told Barbara Cartland, "They won't accept me. Whatever I do is wrong. I just want us to be one close family."

To help pay off some of the immense death duties incurred by the death of the Seventh Earl Spencer, Raine went about revamping the house. She opened the house to the public offering guided tours and had a souvenir shop built in the stable block. She even employed staff to open an afternoon tea bar to encourage the day trippers. All this did not go down too well with the Spencer children.

But then near tragedy brought the family together and the children, even Sarah, began to see another side to Raine. She became literally a lifesaver to their father and all the children had cause to thank her. Just a few days after holding a party celebrating his return to a position of credit at the bank, the Earl collapsed in the stable yard with a massive brain haemorrhage.

He was rushed to Northampton Hospital where doctors told Raine he was unlikely to survive the night. She refused to believe this and immediately chartered a private ambulance to dash seventy miles to a special brain clinic in London. She then began a long fight to save his life, swapping doctors and hospitals in her determination. "I wanted to use my life and my energy for his life," she said later. Sitting beside his bed for hours on end she cajoled and nagged her husband back to life. One day she played him a tape of one of his favourite operas, 'Madame Butterfly,' and quite suddenly he just opened his eyes and came out of a long coma.

He said later that through his coma he had heard everything that Raine had said to him. Now there is little to show for his near brush with death, just a slight blurring of his voice, an occasional speech hesitation. The Spencer girls, who are all devoted to their father, were delighted by what Raine had achieved.

By 1978 Lady Diana, sixteen-years-old and fresh out of West Heath school, was at the exclusive Institut Alpin Videmanette in Rougemont, Switzerland, a very expensive finishing school for young ladies. It was while she was at the school, improving her skiing and learning social poise and grace that her sister was in the same Swiss Alps at Klosters holidaying with Prince Charles.

T HE HOLIDAY was the talk of the Press and the school, but Diana never spoke of it. Diana was improving her already good grasp of the French language and her teacher, Madame Barbara Fuls, recalled that "while Diana was a pretty girl she was not the beauty she's blossomed into now. She knew she wanted to work with children, to get married and have a family of her own, and she once told me that she would only marry for love not for money or position."

During her brief stay at the institute, Diana took domestic science and learned the art of dressmaking and cooking, mainly French or Swiss, certainly not the roast beef of old England. But she did not last the full course in Switzerland. Suffering from a severe bout of homesickness, she returned to Britain after only two months.

Her father decided she should have her freedom and bought her a London flat, the home she was to have for two years until her engagement to Prince Charles. Diana moved in, gathering round her the three girls who were to become her closest friends and confidantes.

Just like her sisters, Diana had decided, despite her social status, she did not want to be a debutante. Becoming a "deb" is the unique English ritual involving the introduction of a young woman into London society. It involves an expensive round of parties, dances and afternoon teas, a tradition with origins deeply rooted in the upper classes.

Diana wanted none of this; instead of being heralded into society she took the job she had always wanted, looking after children in a kindergarten. Her character and her way of life were now well formed and she had grown into a beautiful young woman. She was no longer the giggly schoolgirl Prince Charles remembered.

Diana had developed into a fresh, deceptively unsophisticated girl, warm, reliable, quick witted, open hearted and very attractive. But strangely enough during this time of freedom in one of the liveliest capitals in the world, Diana never had a steady boyfriend. She went out on occasional dates but they were purely platonic friendships.

According to one of her friends, Old Etonian Simon Berry, aged twenty-three, whose parents run a London wine business, Lady Diana broke the hearts of dozens of young men during the two years she lived in Coleherne Court. "Chaps would meet Diana and fall instantly in love," he said. "Many tried to win her, sending flowers and begging for a date, but she always politely declined." Diana was never one for discos or parties.

Occasional meals at her favourite London restaurant, the Poule au Pot in Ebury Street, Victoria, where she would dine with a group, or private dinner parties at the home of friends were the usual way she spent a night out. She seemed to love cosy evenings at home with her friends. She chose her friends very carefully, almost as if she were planning for a future in which her past would be closely examined. All her chosen companions were well bred, well educated and totally trustworthy.

What Diana is instantly remembered for is her tremendous sense of humour. Like Prince Charles, Diana seems to revel in a good practical joke and pranks to be played on her friends like doing impressions of Miss Piggy in the Muppets television series over the telephone. During their brief courtship Charles and Diana would roar with laughter together over a brilliant little send-up of them in the British satirical magazine *Private Eye*. The *Eye* wrote about their romance in a mushy manner under the byline 'Silvie Krin.'

In the regular fortnightly features Diana was always looking at Charles with limpid eyes while he only had evil thoughts on how to deprive her of her virginity. Charles had kept all the issues and together they would read them again and again, delighted by the wicked humour. Like Charles, Diana had acquired a liking for the arts and for music; she plays the piano a little, he the cello. She had learned to love driving, passing her test at the age of eighteen.

Again, like the man she was to marry, she rarely drinks, except for a glass of wine, and she has never smoked. It was her driving which gave a clue to a hitherto unseen side to Lady Diana Spencer. As soon as she passed her test she gained a reputation as a demon driver. She was involved in three minor accidents in the first year she coped with the pressures of the fierce London traffic. Her first car, a light blue Volkswagen Polo, always seemed to be off the road for repairs to a new dent or scrape and photographers chasing her at the start of the Royal courtship discovered that she enjoyed a good snarl at other drivers who were not quick enough for her as she whipped crisply round Central London.

Lady Diana Frances Spencer had grown up to be a woman with a mind of her own as well as a natural beauty. Even before her engagement the much photographed Spencer glossy fringe from which she peeped out shyly at the world was being copied in hair stylists' salons all over Britain. Thousands of young girls have adopted her honey blonde hairstyle.

Although she is a very wealthy young lady, Diana's teenage clothes style was never extravagant. It was not the usual Gucci, Puci and Fiorucci. She was never caught in anything more outré than a pair of corduroy culottes, a borrowed sweatshirt or a man's corduroy smoking jacket. But she is doomed to a life of flat shoes. High heels are out for a girl who is as tall as her fiancé: it wouldn't be protocol to tower over the future King.

WHAT A DAY!

THE WORST-KEPT SECRET IN THE WORLD

THEIR JOY was plain to see: in their eyes, in the way they touched and in the laughter they shared. "Blissfully happy" were the words Diana used, the light sparkling like champagne from her spectacular sapphire and diamond ring. "With Prince Charles beside me I can't go wrong."said the lovely teenager who was telling the world how she would become Princess of Wales and one day Queen of England.

On the steps at the back of Buckingham Palace leading down from a stone flagged terrace which overlooked lovely ornate gardens and a lake, Diana rested her head for a moment against the Prince's neck in a gesture of pure affection. He placed his hands on the shoulders of her vivid blue pure silk suit and they laughed and laughed. High spirited, like a schoolgirl, Lady Diana revealed that she had answered the Royal marriage proposal "straight away."

Diana and her Prince were pouring their hearts out to the world's Press whom they had spent the last six months so studiously avoiding. The time was around noon on 24 February, 1981, and everything was going perfectly. Earlier, sitting side by side on the sofa in the same sitting room where the Prince had asked for her hand in marriage, the couple had given an interview which would enter the history books as one of the frankest ever given by a member of the Royal Family. Then Diana and Charles had undergone an ordeal by television. Two tough TV reporters had grilled them about love and even the twelve-year gap in their ages. The unsophisticated teenager, totally unused, unlike her fiancé, to public appearances had come out as a winner. It was the endless smile of pure happiness on the girl's face that really said what words couldn't and delighted the 500 million viewers round the world who watched that five minute interview.

Prince Charles took the lead as they were interviewed with Lady Diana laughing quietly and at first playing purely a secondary role.

How did they feel?

"Absolutely delighted and frankly amazed that Diana is prepared to take me on," said Prince Charles jocularly.

"Absolutely delighted too, blissfully happy," said Lady Diana.

Lady Diana was asked when they first met. "I first met him in November 1977. Prince Charles came as a friend of my sister Sarah for a shoot. I never saw Prince Charles before 1977. I was always paired with Prince Andrew." She gave one of her nervous giggles.

When did they decide to get engaged? Prince Charles: "It was about three weeks ago, believe it or not, just before Diana went to Australia. She planned to go to Australia quite a long time before anyway and I thought I will ask her then so she will have a chance to think it over so she could say 'I can't bear the whole idea' or not, but she actually accepted."

Lady Diana (with a giggle): "Straight away...There were quite a lot of telephone calls."

Prince Charles: "So many telephone calls from the Press in Australia saying they were Buckingham Palace or me. When I called, the man said 'How do I know who you are?' I said 'Well you don't, but I am,' in a rage. It was quite difficult to keep the secret for three weeks but we managed it."

THE WEDDING date? Prince Charles: "No date as such, but certainly the idea is the latter part of July which is probably the easiest from all sorts of peoples' points of view. We haven't actually fixed the date." He added: "It is much nicer to get married in summer."

The BBC man asked if her might dare ask about the honeymoon. "You can dare," said Prince Charles. "We don't know. There is a lot to be decided and worked out."

Where would they live after the wedding? Prince Charles: "Basically, I hope, down at Highgrove in Gloucestershire. I dare say that means we will have to try and find somewhere in London to have as a base as well, but at the moment Highgrove. There's an awful lot to be done there...marvellous to have someone to take it on, organise everything, because it's completely empty at the moment – I'm just camping out – and there's a great deal to be done isn't there?"

Lady Diana, again with a small laugh, agreed: "Yes."

Asked about being in the public eye, foreign travel and public engagements, Lady Diana said: "Naturally quite daunting, but I hope it won't be too difficult."

Prince Charles said: "I am very much looking forward to meeting lots of different people," and a laughing Lady Diana said: "I am going to have to."

Prince Charles: "When I first started public engagements, I think about the same age really, twenty, it wasn't easy to begin with obviously, but after a bit you do get used to it. You just have to take the plunge. I hope I can help pass on the bit of experience I have." He turned to Lady Diana and said: "You like people which is a great thing."

What about their age difference – he was thirty-one, she is nineteen. "Never really thought about it," said Lady Diana confidently.

"I haven't, I mean, it's only twelve years," said Prince Charles. "Lots of people have got married with that sort of age difference. I always feel you are as old as you think or feel you are. I think Diana will keep me young. That's a very good thing. I shall be exhausted."

After the TV technicians, the still photographers and the reporters had packed up and driven away from the Palace, delighted by what they had in their tape recordings and film cans, the future Princess of Wales found herself in a very strange new world. She would never be able to wander out and have her hair done again as she had earlier that day. She would never be able to pop down to the shops, especially the little late night supermarket she was particularly fond of near her flat, where she would buy her breakfast grapefruit and milk. Worst of all she would never be able to enjoy cosy evenings with her friends left behind at Coleherne Court.

That evening for the first time Lady Diana and Charles were able to get in the same car together without the worry of being spotted. It was the end of months of secret meetings in country estates with high walls and long drives. They were able to proclaim their love for everyone to see. Diana had changed into a full length skirt and a simple gown, her Prince was in an evening jacket and bow tie and Diana was still flashing that stunning ring she was so proud of. It was only a 500 yard drive to Diana'a new home at Clarence House, there to have dinner with the Queen Mother and her Lady-in-Waiting, Lady Fermoy, who is Diana's grandmother. It was a wonderfully relaxed evening after a day that had gone off so perfectly. Diana was even trying out a sort of regal wave for the first time, smiling and turning to a group of elderly women Royalists who had braved the cold to stand outside Clarence House singing 'Congratulations and Jubilations' to the tune of a once popular hit song by Cliff Richard. It was a fairytale way for a Prince to announce that he had found his lady at last.

The announcement of their wedding brought the vital news of joy that Britain, and perhaps the world, needed at a time of gloom. President Reagan and British Prime Minister, Margaret Thatcher, were just about to meet in Washington for the first time to discuss problems that spread from massive unemployment not only in their own countries, but throughout the world.

Armaments, more tanks, more troops, higher defence budgets were being talked about both in Washington, London and Moscow. Détente was not working out – and new men both in Moscow and Washington were deciding on how they would face up to each other. For the superpowers there was trouble spreading from Afghanistan to South America, Middle East tension and Far Eastern chaos and for the people relying on the world leaders to sort out the mess, the main task each day was finding enough work and money either to buy gas for the car or a loaf of bread, depending on which hemisphere they lived.

In Britain a potentially disastrous miners' strike was at hand. Then, at eleven o'clock on a spring-like morning enormous joy was brought into the world with a handsome young couple holding hands and hugging each other on the green lawns of a huge private house in the centre of London. Sure there were more matters of import to face the world – but here, at last, was joy. A reminder to everyone, no matter what religion, political view or regime that love still existed. There was still cause for happiness. President Reagan and his wife, Nancy, heard the news on TV over breakfast in the White House. "Ronnie and I are absolutely delighted," said the First Lady. "I have never met Lady Diana but I have met her stepmother and I know they are a marvellous family."

CANADIAN PREMIER Pierre Trudeau said, according to a spokesman, "Everybody is pleased, excited and elated."

The rumours had been going the rounds of Britain's newspaper capital, for at least six months, but, when, at last, they could burst forth, the editorials let fly with the joy that reflected the reaction of most of the nation.

The traditionalist *Daily Express*, which has always been a defender of the Commonwealth and Royalty opinioned robustly under the headline 'ROYAL RAY OF SUNSHINE – it may have been the worst kept secret in the world, but nothing will detract from the Royal Family on the engagement of Prince Charles to Lady Diana Spencer.'

His Royal Highness could not have made a better choice for a future Queen of England. She was British through and through and from a family of historical distinction and numerous Royal links. A Royal Engagement and a summer wedding could not have come at a better time. The mundane facts of British life were pretty grim. The dreary statistics of unemployment and falling production, strikes and threats of strikes, had depressed for far too long.

What better than a Royal Romance to warm and cheer all our hearts? All the world loves a love story and this was the premier love story of the decade. It was an occasion of a genuine national celebration.

Another royalist and traditionalist publication, the *Daily Mail* remarked 'Some Princes do have all the luck' then commented: 'At last, it is to be Royal Wedding bells. And we are delighted for them both. Prince Charles is a very lucky man. He has played the field and led the ladies a merry dance. And now he has been accepted by a lovely girl, who still has the freshness of the morning dew. Ah well, what's the point in being Prince of Wales if he can't do that? Dull of heart, indeed, must the citizen be who does not share in the happiness of Prince Charles and Lady Diana. Yesterday the whole nation seemed to be smiling.'

The *Daily Mirror* said: 'Now we can look forward to a summer wedding. The bride will be radiant, the bridesmaids beautiful, the mothers tearful, the Prince, charming, of course. And on the day we'll forget our problems for a while. Hoperfully the sun will shine and even if it doesn't, who will care? We'll celebrate a splendid British occasion: a Royal marriage. The greatest show on earth.'

The ultra-respectable *Economist* said: 'The Monarchy is the British institution that still works, chiefly because the British have learned when, and when not, to take it too seriously. While foreign republicans have to rally in moments of patriotic emotion round heads of state who – nearly half the population may be simultaneously shrieking – should be sent to prison for burgling Watergate or accepting diamonds from a cannibal chief, the British entrust the unifying role in national policy to a family supposed to derive its authority as head of British morality from its inalienable birthright...'

Then, referring to that great authority on not only British but world-wide monarchies, it went on: 'Debrett has discovered that Lady Diana Spencer descends five times from King Charles II, although four times from the wrong side of the blanket; but the real point is that British Monarchy works well because its blue blood is constantly diluted by charm and fun.'

There had to be at least one sour note, of course, and this came from the Communist *Morning Star* whose main circulation is beyond the Iron Curtain. In what, one hopes, was a tongue-in-cheek article it reported under the headline 'DON'T DO IT LADY DIANA: Lady Diana Spencer is to sacrifice her independence to a domineering layabout for the sake of a few lousy foreign holidays. As the future Queen of England she can expect a fair bit of first class travel and a lot of attention, but with a £100,000 home of her own and a steady job as an exclusive nursery nurse, who needs it?'

It could not have pleased the *Morning Star* editorialists later that day either when the capitalist trading on the London Stock Exchange went up a few points with news of the engagement and the pound strengthened on the international money markets. Obviously everyone loves lovers – even Zurich bankers. And in the same way that what is good for General Motors is supposed to be good for America, the prospect of a Royal Wedding was obviously good for Britain.

ON THE London stock market there was a rush to buy shares in firms likely to cash in on the rush for souvenirs or in the hotel business. Shares which had been sluggish the day before leapt dramatically. Hopes that the celebrations would pull in more American tourists boosted the shares of hotels group Trust House Forte by 7p to 200p a share. China manufacturers Royal Worcester, famous for their commemorative plates and mugs, jumped 23p a share to 293p. Pottery and tableware group Wedgwood also put on 5p, while Birmingham Mint, famous for commemorative silver and gold medallions, jumped 17p to 223p.

Mr. Roy Stephens, managing director of Selfridges, summed up the feelings of London's store owners. He said: "It is good news for us because it will bring in a lot of foreign visitors." A million extra visitors were immediately expected to pour into Britain from all over the world for the Royal Wedding, making it a record year for the tourist trade. An English Tourist Board spokesman said: "You probably won't be able to get beds in London for love or money before and after the wedding day."

The souvenir trade was likely to beat the record sales during the Queen's Silver Jubilee four years ago when there was a boom in the sales of everything from tea cups to bath-towels, provided they had the Royal Crest or the Queen's head on them. By the afternoon of the engagement announcement, towels, scarves, crockery and silverware, and hundreds of other items which some shrewd businessmen had held back in warehouses hoping with fingers crossed that Lady Diana was the one, were being distributed throughout Britain by fleets of speeding trucks.

The leading soothsayers of the stars, the astrologers, also had their share of the action. "Charles and Diana are a good love match," said one of Britain's leading experts in the field, Russell Grant. "The Prince is Scorpio and his bride-to-be Cancer. Their sun signs are as compatible as love and marriage. It's the beginning of one of the most electrifying marriages ever."

Even a computer decided that they were ideally suited. It also predicted their marriage is the one most likely to last. The analysis was made by Dateline Computer Dating – the biggest computer matchmakers in Britain. Information on Charles and bride-to-be was fed into the computer and it returned the highest compatibility rating possible. They were said to be ideally matched on scores of interests and hobbies ranging from sports to politics and romance.

So now we know...

HOMES, SWEET HOMES

FROM EARLS COURT TO HIGHGROVE

UNTIL HER marriage, homes for the former Lady Diana Spencer meant Park House on the Royal Estate at Sandringham in Norfolk where she was born, Althorp, her family's ancestral stately mansion in North-amptonshire where she spent her adolescence, the Isle of Seil in Scotland where she holidayed with her divorced mother, and the crowded shared flat at 60 Coleherne Court in West London, just a few minutes walk from her favourite Knightsbridge shops.

Now, five years into her marriage, she has two official homes of her own. Later she will inherit, or be given, other mansions and as Queen will be mistress of more houses, castles and places than any other woman in the world.

But she wasn't exactly excited the day she saw her million-pound country home in Gloucester-shire for the first time in October 1980. Prince Charles had gone househunting during the months of July and August, during an odd period in his life following the break-up of his affair with lovely blonde Anna Wallace.

Diana was not then part of his life. In fact, the Prince wasn't escorting anyone when he decided to buy the first-ever home of his own. He asked the trustees who manage his inheritance, the Duchy of Cornwall estates in West England, to find him a suitable place. He gave only the briefest of instructions – not too big or grand, plenty of land and, hopefully, near good hunting country.

In August, clutching a glossy, full-colour estate agent's brochure, Charles turned his midnight-blue Ford Granada off the A453, through a set of rusting wrought-iron gates and crunched his way up a half mile tarmac and gravel drive. This was the Prince's first sight of Highgrove, set in 347 acres of beautiful Cotswold countryside. "Perfect," the Prince told estate agents, Humberts, and several weeks later Highgrove was his. It was geographically perfect for a man who was busy, sociable and sporting: 90 miles of easy motorway driving from London, and even handier for Windsor Castle. He found that visiting his family for Windsor weekends would only take about an hour without breaking any speed limits.

His sister Princess Anne, and her husband

Captain Mark Phillips, were less than 10 miles down the road at Gatcombe Park. Cheltenham was handy for the races and Cirencester for the polo. Highgrove was in Beaufort Hunt country and Badminton, scene of the major cross-country horse trials, was a neighbouring mansion. Down there in the Cotswolds, reasoned the Prince, he was within reach of the Duchy of Cornwall, thousands of acres of prime land which were his birthright and his income.

Unfortunately, although the outside of the Georgian house, once the home of Maurice Macmillan, a Conservative member of Parliament and son of the former Prime Minister, was reasonably attractive, facing north and adorned with magnolia and clinging wisteria, the interior was a sorry sight. Charles needed a female viewpoint on what he considered to be a rare find in the English countryside. So came a day in October when Diana, still a teenager, and never dreaming she would one day share this home as his wife, drove down with him for her first look. She was the first of his lady friends to lay eyes on Highgrove and to her standards the house, built in 1763 but later substantially refurbished, was a small one. Her father's huge red brick Elizabethan manor, Althorp, 160 miles further north near the industrial city of Northampton, was far grander.

Althorp contained one of the finest private art collections in Europe, and was so big that the public could be taken round on guided tours without disruption to normal life, for the Spencer family lived in just one wing. Highgrove would have fitted neatly into the area covered by Althorp's staff flats and outbuildings.

Members of Prince Charles' household who were present at Highgrove when Diana saw her future home, revealed later that the lady was far from impressed. She didn't say a word after she climbed the wide easy-tread staircase to the master bedroom, then known as the yellow room, dominated with a giant double bed complete with flowery satin covered headboard.

She wandered through the eight other bedrooms and three bathrooms showing particular interest in the two-room wing which had been used as a nursery by the Macmillan family. She may not have said a word but her face told it all.

To be fair, Highgrove was a mess, half-decorated, half-furnished, with only three usable bedrooms. The Prince enjoyed what he termed "roughing it" in this unpretentious and at that time, unappealing, house. The future Princess probably thought that her own place at that time, the first floor three-bedroomed shared flat in Earls Court, untidy, scattered with clothes, sometimes with tennis racquets, skis and even bicycles parked in the hall, and busy with boyfriends, was far more homely.

But rundown and unattractive as it was, Highgrove was where the Prince and Lady Diana did their courting...it was one of the few places where they could really be alone together in a world where their love had to remain a secret. They camped out at weekends, looked after by a detective, a valet, Stephen Barry, and two elderly retainers who used to work for the Macmillan family, now part of the official Royal Highgrove household, Paddy and Nesta Whitehead.

After the engagement was announced Diana took it on herself to redecorate what was to be their first married home. She made dozens of trips up and down the M4 from London turning gloomy old Highgrove into a beautiful and comfortable retreat for herself, the Prince and their future family. She kept most of the work a secret from Charles, who kept away as teams of workmen swarmed over the property completing the transformation. He did not see the finished product until after their honeymoon in Scotland when the Princess, in a state of high excitement, showed him around every room.

He loved it, and today Highgrove is where they spend the majority of their family life together despite criticism from inside the Royal Family that it isn't big enough and doesn't afford enough privacy. A footpath has been moved making it difficult for peeping toms to watch them at play.

The Princess has strong and highly individual ideas about interior decoration. At Coleherne Court she painted the sitting-room walls primrose yellow, and decorated the bathroom with wallpaper covered in red cherries. But by the time she became mistress of Highgrove she had also become a little more sophisticated.

She had the spacious hall rag-rolled pink, in keeping with the Georgian style. The green drawing room has attractive fringed curtains, and there are now many polished wooden floors in her house. The kitchen and the butler's pantry have been re-equipped with a hundred units, given to them as a £10,000 wedding present, and the nursery decorated with murals starring fairytale characters.

The garden she left strictly to Charles. It includes a superbly maintained formal area dominated by a magnificent cedar of Lebanon, cut-leaf beech and tulip trees set among the carefully clipped lawns and well pruned rosebeds. Charles and Diana went to the Chelsea Flower Show unannounced to pick prize shrubs and roses for their garden.

A swimming pool was built behind the house from money collected by thousands of soldiers, a wedding present from the British Army. It is there that Prince William and now Prince Harry are learning to swim, and where Diana takes her

Turn to page 113

When speculation about her relationship with Prince Charles was at its height in the autumn of 1980, Lady Diana Spencer, then just 19 years of age, found herself followed almost every day by newsmen and photographers from her flat in Kensington to the Pimlico kindergarten where she worked (left). But she accepted the Press and public interest with good humour and admirable self control. (Above) Lady Diana returning to her flat after an evening with Prince Charles.

On the day of their engagement, the 24th of February 1981, Prince Charles and his fiancée posed for photographs on the front lawns of Buckingham Palace. Lady Diana's engagement ring was made of diamonds and sapphires.

Happy informality was brilliantly caught in these superb photographs of Prince Charles and his fiancée by Snowdon (above and left). (Right) The first picture of the newly-engaged couple with her Majesty the Queen in the drawing room of Buckingham Palace. (Overleaf) A touch of majesty – Lady Diana Spencer's youthful but regal bearing captured at Highgrove House, their future country residence, with Prince Charles. It was their first official portrait as bride and groom-to-be.

A recital in aid of the Royal Opera House development Appeal at Goldsmiths' Hall, London, on the 3rd of March 1981 was Lady Diana's first official function. Her revealing black taffeta evening dress caused a sensation. Another Royal guest at the recital was the late Princess Grace of Monaco.

Before the wedding, Lady Diana Spencer visited Broadlands (top left) where she was to spend the first days of her honeymoon, and, with Prince Charles, the village of Tedbury (bottom left), two miles from her future home, Highgrove House, to meet her neighbours. (Above left) Lady Diana was full of smiles when she visited Cheltenham and surprised everybody (right) with her red saucer-shaped hat while attending the wedding of Nicholas Soames to Miss Catherine Wetherhall at St Margaret's with Prince Charles and Princess Margaret. (Right) Lady Diana attended her first polo match at Smith's Lawn, Windsor, accompanied by Prince Charles and Prince Andrew.

Lady Diana took her first carriage drive to Ascot with her fiancé Prince Charles (left) and immediately started a new fashion trend at Ascot, where she mingled happily with the crowds. (Above) A change of fashions: country living will be an important part in Princess Diana's life, and before her wedding she showed her fiancé that she could dress suitably with warm and colourful sweaters and cords.

THE WEDDING OF THE CENTURY
The Royal Wedding which was to be seen on television worldwide by an audience of more than 600 million gets under way. The first of the Royal Carriages makes its way to the St Paul's for the ceremony. (Overleaf) Lady Diana Spencer's carriage carries her to her wedding to Prince Charles.

On the arm of her father, the Earl Spencer, Lady Diana begins her slow measured walk to where Prince

Charles awaits her. Her full 25-ft long train stretches out behind her as she makes her way up the nave.

The wedding ceremony gets under way, conducted by Dr Robert Runcie, the Archbishop of Canterbury, in the architectural splendour of St Paul's Cathedral. (and next six pages)

The journey back from St Paul's Cathedral was triumphant, the cheers deafening. The new Princess was the darling of the vast crowds and with an escort of Life Guards. (Overleaf)

she responded modestly but with evident delight. The Prince of Wales and his new bride were driven in the 1902 State Postillion Landau, The State Landau in The Mall.

From the Balcony of Buckingham Palace, The Prince and Princess of Wales acknowledge the persistent acclamations from almost three-quarters of a million people who had surged towards the Palace to welcome a new Princess of Wales, the first since 1863.

(Above) The Prince of Wales kisses The Princess of Wales' hand and **(right)** more jubilant scenes on the balcony. **(Overleaf)** History was created when, after asking The Queen's permission, The Prince of Wales kisses his bride in public – to the delight of the crowds.

Prince Charles and Princess Diana with Prince Andrew, Prince Edward,

the Pages and Maids of Honour, pose for this charming wedding picture.

This family group picture, to commemorate the union of the Prince and Princess of Wales was taken

at Buckingham Palace by Lord Patrick Lichfield. (Overleaf) A bow from Prince Charles to his bride.

Charming wedding photographs of The Prince and Princess of Wales for the Royal Picture Album.

LEAVING ON HONEYMOON (and overleaf). Late in the afternoon they left Buckingham Palace, hotly pursued by relatives and retainers with confetti, in a carriage bedecked with blue and silver balloons and a "**JUST MARRIED**" notice stuck on the back. The newlyweds were en-route to Waterloo Station where a train was to take them to Romsey on the first stage of their honeymoon.

The Prince and Princess of Wales boarded Her Majesty's Yacht Britannia in Gibraltar for a long Mediterranean honeymoon that was to take them to the Greek Islands and Egypt. They waved to the crowds as Britannia was leaving the Rock.

Her Majesty's yacht Britannia, with the Prince and Princess of Wales on Board, receives an enthusiastic welcome at Port Said, Egypt.

The Royal Yacht Britannia sailed
through the Suez Canal with Prince
Charles and Princess Diana
sunbathing on deck and admiring the
view, as hundreds of Egyptian Soldiers
guarded both banks.
Princess Diana wore a yellow bikini
during the slow voyage along the canal,
but retreated indoors when the ship
reached Suez where the couple were
greeted by a horde of Press
photographers.
After a few days sailing, Britannia
finally reached the South of Egypt
where, following a farewell to the
officers of their Egyptian escort ship,
the Prince and Princess of Wales
boarded a flight back to London.

The splendid Scottish countryside provided the best pictures of the honeymoon. The Prince and Princess of Wales are seen here strolling in the heather and posing by the side of the River Dee in the grounds of Balmoral Castle, which they will one day inherit. (and the next four pages)

Princess Diana's hairstyle was to change dramatically from the time of her engagement (top left) to the present. Previous styles were to be copied by millions of young women the world over, all awaiting new pictures of the Princess to mimic any change.

Hats, thanks to Princess Diana, are back in fashion creating a boom in the millinery industry. Diana has a vast number of different styles, each new one quickly mass produced on the world market as soon as it appears.

Prince Charles' expression shows his happiness and pride in his wife at an evening function. Princess Diana once again dazzled with her simple but elegant fashions.

Princess Diana has become the most photographed woman in the world. The No. 1 cover girl appears on the front of magazines more often than any other princess or movie star. The Press and public alike never tire of her.

Prince Charles often seems dazzled by his wife's beautiful evening dresses (left) and, as our picture shows, is sometimes openly surprised by the very personal choice favoured by Princess Diana.

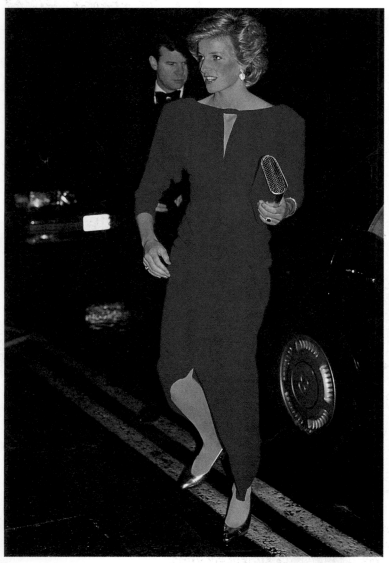

Princess Diana has brought back glamour and style to the world of fashion with her tremendous influence, particularly where her huge wardrobe of fabulous evening dresses is concerned. The Princess caused a sensation when she experimented with a new way of wearing a necklace, in order to enhance the plunge backline of her dress.

It is not difficult to understand how proud Prince Charles is of his wife's exceptional taste and style in clothes. This pride and admiration is constantly reflected to the world's Press whenever the couple appear in public together.

It was fashion of a different kind when Princess Diana revealed her maternity wardrobe first to the people of the Scilly Isles (top left) and at Smith's Lawn, Windsor (bottom left and above) when watching her husband play polo. Overleaf, a radiant and blooming Princess Diana a few months before the birth of her first child, Prince William.

Continued from page 32

morning exercise. Charles is said to prefer the garden to the pool, even going to the lengths of digging out a vegetable plot and growing his own salads and new potatoes.

He has turned Highgrove into a working farm, and always keen on conservation, everything on the estate is organically grown. There are no chemicals at Highgrove. It was this near-obsession with Highgrove and family life that led to rows inside the Family, and led to the ticking-off he received from his father, who considered his public workload to be more important than his vegetable garden.

There is no doubt that marriage and Highgrove have made Charles a happy man, even if he had to hang up his gardening boots for longer than he cares for the formal attire of public appearances.

In London the couple's official residence is in the northwest part of Kensington Palace, overlooking Kensington Green. Their address is apartments Eight and Nine, and their neighbours are Prince and Princess Michael of Kent. Numbers Eight and Nine were damaged by German bombs during World War II and remained burned out and derelict until 1975.

There were structural alterations and redecoration when the wedding was announced in 1981, but the apartments were not quite ready when the couple returned from honeymoon, so they lived at Highgrove.

They use Kensington Palace during the week while they are carrying out their official engagements because of its convenience to their work. Queen Victoria was the last British Monarch to live in Kensington Palace. She was constantly supervised by her mother, Princess Victoire, and grew up in what are now the State Apartments, sleeping in the same bed as her mother.

She was barely 18 when she became Queen, and one of her first acts was to provide herself with a bedroom and a single bed in which she slept on her own for the first time. A few weeks later the teenage Queen moved into Buckingham Palace.

Charles and Diana's London home takes up three storeys in Prince of Wales Court at Kensington Palace. They are connected by four flights of a fine Georgian staircase, which largely survived the bombing. The rooms were decorated by South African interior designer Dudley Poplak. There is a double drawing room with flock wallpaper, a sitting room for the Princess and a study for the Prince. Strangely, there are two downstairs cloakrooms, a "His" and "Her's" for the use of guests. In "His" framed newspaper cartoons lampooning Charles hang on the walls, the Prince himself deciding that this was the best place for this lavatory humour.

There is a dining room, a master bedroom with a new bathroom *en-suite*, marbled and mirrored; two guest bedrooms, a nursery suite with separate nearby bedroom for the nanny to be on instant call; a breakfast room with an adjoining music room, and rooms for staff.

The roof contains a brick barbeque which the Princess, much to the envy of her sun-worshipping neighbour, Princess Michael, cleverly had made into a picturesque and very private green garden hideaway overlooking Kensington Green public gardens. Diana can see the joggers and strollers as she sits in the sunshine, but the thousands who use the park every day can't see her. Privacy at Kensington Palace is complete, for it offers complete security. The buildings, at the end of a long drive, are easy to guard, and there is a permanent and well-armed 24-hour police presence. Complex alarm systems and secret "panic" buttons in many of the rooms enable the Prince or Princess to summon instant help should the need arise.

UNFORTUNATELY things are more difficult at Highgrove, for the house is a policeman's nightmare. It is surrounded by public rights of way, and can be clearly seen from the main road. At night, car headlights must be visible from the bedroom windows, although fast-growing fir trees have been planted for extra privacy. When the Prince bought the house, cottages in the grounds were turned into homes for the resident police guard, and much of the glass was replaced with a thick, bullet-proof variety.

The same "panic" button system Buckingham Palace now enjoys was installed, and it is said that a steel-walled room has been built inside to protect the family against any kind of attack, including rocket and gas. Highgrove is not as secluded, commodious and attractive as the residence of a future King and Queen should be. A house and home like Althorp would be ideal. Perhaps one day Charles will build a new home for his Princess, as Queen Victoria's eldest son did at Sandringham 100 years ago.

Charles and Diana did not have the usual problem faced by most newlyweds – how to furnish their two homes. Their problem was a writing one, the sheer monotonous grind of putting their joint names to the bottom of thousands of *"Thank You"* notes to the people who sent them wedding presents, furniture, bed linen, beautiful cut-glass, paintings, and priceless jewellery.

THEY took it in turns, Diana using a blue pen and her husband a black one to write *"Yours Most Sincerely"* on each typed letter to people from all over the world who had furnished their new homes.

The same letters went out, whether to a Saudi Arabian Royal Family in thanks for diamonds and sapphires, or a grandmother from Leicester for a pressed flower in a wedding card. Rich or poor, famous or unknown, whatever the gift, the Royal thank you note was the same.

The thousands of wedding presents were catalogued and their value estimated. When they went on show at St. James's Palace they were insured for £4,000,000 but this is well below their true worth. Since then other presents have now been revealed, and it is clear that Prince Charles and his wife, two very wealthy people in their own right, received an astonishing £11,000,000 worth of gifts.

Amongst them was a stunning diamond necklace, ring and earrings from the heir apparent of the State of Qatar, a solid gold and diamond encrusted model of an Arab fishing boat from the Emir of the State of Bahrain, more diamonds from the United Arab Emirates, pearls from Fiji, ivory from Nigeria, more gold and diamonds from Thailand, priceless rare carpets from India, and endless gifts of silver from all over the world.

A cut glass vase from the Reagans in the White House is said to be worth £40,000. Many of the really ostentatious Arab sparklers were never put on public display. They went straight to Buckingham Palace to disappear into the vaults. Valuable gifts to the Queen from the Middle East countries are not at all unusual. In return the Queen and Prince Philip usually send a signed framed photograph of themselves.

There were other gifts never officially announced, like the two fully fitted kitchens donated by two rival German firms, now installed at Highgrove, one in the house, the other in a cottage; a £7,000 grand piano was sent to Kensington Palace, although the firm which gave it away was warned that the Prince does not play.

When Socialist MPs began questioning the ethics of wealthy people accepting such free gifts, a Buckingham Palace spokesman would only counter with: "Why shouldn't they accept them? All the gifts were sent in good faith." One though, an expensive collection of babywear and nursery furniture, was sent back with an angry phone call from a member of the Royal Household after allegations that the firm which sent the presents were trying to get publicity for their baby boutique. Buckingham Palace, pleased to accept valuable gifts, frowned on people "cashing in" on the Royal Couple.

Most of those thousands of presents have now disappeared for ever into the Royal homes. If their fate is anything like the sad end to some of the presents sent to the Queen when she married Prince Philip, more basements at Buckingham Palace are likely to be filled to overflowing.

Shortly before their wedding, the Queen invited Diana to take a look in those cavernous basements with an instruction to help herself to anything which took her fancy in the furniture line. In these rooms, Diana later told friends, were unopened packing cases, fine furniture covered with dustsheets, and endless oil paintings – all gifts the Queen and Prince Philip had no use for. Diana described it as a "treasure trove" and soon servants were taking her booty by van down to Gloucestershire.

DYNASTY

THE ORIGINAL ANXIOUS FATHER

PRINCE CHARLES once said "A marriage is not only for the two people who are forming the marriage. It is also for the children." He made this profound statement in his bachelor period, long before Diana came into his life, but even then his views on family life had been moulded. By 33 he had been godfather to a whole nursery of upper-crust children, sons and daughters of family and friends, and he wanted his own children for emotional as well as dynastic reasons, even if the haste with which his young bride did become pregnant so soon after the wedding, did leave him feeling, in his own words, a "little shell-shocked."

Charles became the original anxious father, pacing the floor and offering his bride advice on her condition. Ex-nursery school teacher Diana, well briefed and trained in the art of bringing up baby, didn't want it and told him so. These intimate glimpses into marital life at Highgrove and Kensington Palace would not have come to the surface but for Diana's embarrassing (for Charles) habit of speaking her mind in public.

She was soon to learn the art of not saying anything which might be turned into a newspaper headline, but then, so soon after the honeymoon, the new Princess still had a lot to learn. At her last public appearance before the birth of her first child she told an onlooker in London's dockland that her husband had been buying lots of books about pregnancy.

In whispered confidence to a woman she had never met before the Princess added. "Charles keeps giving me lots of advice" and then rather pointedly "and I can tell you I don't like it." The Prince put away his childbirth books and let Royal gynaecologist, Mr. George Pinker, handle things. Nevertheless, Prince Charles became a new kind of Royal father, going to childbirth classes with his wife and determined to be in at the birth and shoulder his share as a parent.

Strangely enough, although Diana's first pregnancy was greeted with delight by the Royal Family, the happy event was to disrupt some carefully-laid plans. The problem was that no one, not even Charles and Diana, had calculated on a baby so early in their marriage. They had planned to have babies, of course. "Three is the absolute minimum," Diana had told her friends.

She was still on honeymoon when she realised she might be expecting and, bursting with excitement and dying to tell someone, she laid a few plans of her own to hide her happiness until she was absolutely sure. It was the second week in October, 1981. Diana and Charles were enjoying the third month of their extended honeymoon in the peace and quiet of the Scottish Highlands. The autumn days were spent walking, fishing and, unfortunately for the Princess's public image, stag-hunting. But the controversy which surrounded her rifle shot which is said to have killed a fine stag was soon to be forgotten in the wave of national pride and happiness at the event yet to be announced.

On October 12th a surreptitious phone call was made from Balmoral Castle to the London home of Mr. Pinker. The next day, Diana, accompanied only by her personal detective, drove to Aberdeen Airport to catch the regular British Airways flight to Heathrow. Officially it was announced that the Princess had come to London to do some shopping and to visit Highgrove, the Gloucestershire home she and Charles would be moving into later that month. The Highgrove part of her visit was correct but the "shopping" explanation was to cover up a secret visit to the surgery of Mr. Pinker, a quietly-spoken, kindly man whose craggy good looks and greying temples are in the romantic tradition of the fictional family doctor.

He was the youngest man ever to be appointed gynaecologist to the Queen in 1973, quickly earning the nickname of Royal Deliverer after taking care of Princess Anne's two children, Princess Michael of Kent's family and the Duchess of Gloucester's babies. His caring attitude inspired Diana with total confidence; after all, he had brought seven Royal children into the world.

After tests were completed by him, Mr. Pinker told the Princess that her hopes had been realised and she was indeed pregnant. Diana broke the news to Charles on his return to Balmoral from Liverpool, where he had been carrying out two days of official engagements. He was delighted and so was the Queen and the rest of the Royal Family who were told as they gathered for dinner at Balmoral.

But the coming event created more than a few headaches for the Civil Servants and diplomats who plan Royal engagements. After the Christmas that year it was to have been announced from Buckingham Palace that the Prince and Princess of Wales would tour the Commonwealth, allowing millions of loyal subjects the chance to see the Princess for the first time.

The couple were to have flown to Australia then New Zealand and finally Canada. Planning for such a complex 45,000-mile tour had started that autumn, and all those plans and arrangements had to be cancelled. News of the pregnancy was announced by Buckingham Palace on November 5th. Prince Charles said Diana was "overjoyed" – and even that was probably an understatement.

By then, Diana's love of children was well known to the world – her only job after leaving school was to become a teacher at a London kindergarten, where she enjoyed her work looking after toddlers each day. A baby of her own was exactly what she wanted. Even before the wedding she had planned to turn special areas of their two homes, Highgrove and Kensington Palace, into nurseries. In both, two rooms were set aside and Diana ordered colours of blue and gold with matching drapes. For Diana their decoration and arrangement took pride of place over the rest of her home furnishings.

The young Princess, still going through the honeymoon period and only slowly adjusting to her new life, protected by the power and prestige of the Royal Family, now faced the physical problems and changes brought on by her pregnancy. Life had altered so much in so short a time for this once carefree girl, who suddenly found that having babies wasn't all "super fun." She suffered from morning sickness and confided in her ex-flatmates that it was "absolute hell." It was a difficult time as she tried to adjust to her new role and keep up public appearances while feeling "absolutely dreadful," as she put it. But the sickness passed and the Princess bloomed with the growing signs of her pregnancy.

Diana now saw motherhood as a chance to give to her child the happiness she had been denied as the victim of a broken home, where gentleness and concern for each other came to a hurtful end for her parents. She was young and bewildered by the mockery of her schoolfriends as the newspapers revelled in the upper class, bitterly-fought divorce case, when her father sued her mother for adultery. This is believed to be one of the reasons why Diana is so fond of children herself, and why the warmth of a happy family life means so much to her.

She knew how other Royal babies were brought up in isolated nurseries with the offspring getting only the occasional glimpse of their parents. Diana was determined, right from the start, that things would be different for her baby. She was prepared to fight Royal Family traditions, red tape and bureaucracy. Even her husband would try and dictate to her these were early days and a holiday was planned to get away from it all.

All through his bachelor years the Prince had been a great holidaymaker. He always managed to fit in at least three foreign jaunts a year, not counting his official overseas tours, his regular fishing holiday in Scotland and the New Year pheasant shoot at Sandringham. Best of all the Prince enjoyed his winter sports holidays. He had been taught to ski like a professional by the Royal Marines and every January for the past eight years he had flown to Switzerland to spend twelve or thirteen days on the pistes. He always went to the same spot, Klosters in Switzerland, a quiet and exclusive mountain village, and stayed in a rented chalet.

This was where he had taken Diana's sister, Lady Sarah, on a skiing holiday which was later described as "completely platonic." Of course that was long before he met Diana and very much in the past, as the Royal Family, including Charles and Diana, met to spend the New Year celebrations of 1982 at Sandringham House in Norfolk.

Before she became pregnant, Prince Charles had wanted Diana to go with him to Klosters. Diana had learned to ski at school, and he was prepared to give up tearing down the dangerous black runs he usually favoured, to ski with his wife on more sedate slopes. But the pregnancy ruled out any chances of Diana skiing, and she made it quite clear that she wasn't going to sit around all day while Charles did so. Mr. Pinker could see that Diana was feeling a little depressed. "Quite normal," he told the Princess, and it was he who suggested that old family standby – a holiday. Charles would have loved to have gone skiing, but that would hardly have been any fun for Diana, so he came up with the idea of an island in the sun.

Several times in the past the Prince had spent wonderfully carefree holidays on the tiny, isolated island of Windemere in the Bahamas. It was an ideal spot, a real paradise island in the warm waters of the Caribbean, and Charles had always stayed at a cottage owned by the Mountbatten family. Windemere, with its peace, quiet and sunshine, and even more important its privacy, seemed just the place. A holiday was arranged. The owner of the cottage, Lord Romsey and his wife, Penelope, were invited along to make up a happy holiday foursome. The Romseys and the Royal Couple had become close friends as well as a familiar part of the family since the wedding.

Norton Romsey, a cousin of Prince Charles, gave the Prince and Princess his home in Hampshire for the first couple of days of their honeymoon. Charles and Diana had picked a romantic four-poster bed in which to spend their first married night together at the Broadlands Estate, near Romsey, Hampshire. Tactfully, Norton and Penelope had moved out of their home, leaving Charles and Diana alone, except

for two servants. In the Windemere cottage, too, there was another four-poster awaiting them, but this room was even more romantic, with a view through french windows on to white sands and a warm blue sea.

At Sandringham, the Princess was growing tense and more depressed. Twice, as the Prince carried on the endless pheasant shoots, she went off by herself to wander across the snow-covered Norfolk fields to her birthplace, Park House, which is part of the Sandringham Royal estate. Park House held happy memories for Diana because this was the only home she shared with her parents during the good part of their marriage. Diana was only six, and her younger brother just three years old the day their mother Frances "disappeared" from home one day in 1967. It was the end of the Spencer's thirteen-year marriage which had begun, like Diana's would fourteen years later, in a blaze of glory at Westminster Abbey, rather than St. Paul's Cathedral, but with the Queen Elizabeth and Prince Philip among the guests.

Diana was quickly dispatched from her King's Lynn nursery school to a nearby preparatory school, Riddlesworth Hall, near Diss, wearing the regulation grey shorts and maroon jersey. Although she may have been perplexed by her parents' separation, Diana continued to spend much of her school holidays flitting between the two sides.

Perhaps it was these traumatic memories which so depressed Diana, the new bride walking alone in the snow. Charles came to the rescue with first-class seats on a British Airways flight to Nassau for the Romseys, Diana and himself (booked under the names of Mr. and Mrs. Hardy) and one detective.

Diana still looked glum when the group left Heathrow for Nassau, but the first touch of the hot sun put the smile back on her face. Sadly the holiday turned into a bit of a nightmare for Charles and Diana, and angered the Queen.

Just before Christmas the Queen had called British newspaper editors to Buckingham Palace for a chat. "I'd like to request that my daughter-in-law be given a little privacy, gentlemen," was the message. That influential group returned to their offices having offered assurances about Diana, and issued their own instructions to the Royal watchers, the reporters and photographers who followed the couple everywhere. Over Christmas and the New Year they were ordered to keep away from Sandringham. There would be no pictures of a snow Princess. The Queen had been upset by the photographers who had infested the little village of Tetbury, near Charles and Diana's country home, Highgrove, waiting to snatch a photograph of Diana out shopping for her favourite wine gums, chocolates and women's weekly magazines. "She can't even go shopping without being pestered," said the Queen to the editors.

But one national newspaper editor did not dutifully attend to drink the Royal spirit being poured out while the Monarch asked for assurances on her daughter-in-law's privacy. Kelvin Mackenzie, editor of *The Sun*, specialising in photographs of bare-breasted young girls, was determined that his readers should see as much of the Princess of Wales as possible. He wasn't going to make any deal with the Palace, and his readers were going to see a lot more of Diana than they could have imagined.

So when Charles booked those air tickets a similar booking was made on an earlier flight for a *Sun* reporter and photographer. Through the Fleet Street grapevine the editor of another paper, *The Star*, heard about this and, worried for his own circulation if *The Sun* did get any sensational photographs of Diana, immediately dispatched a team to the Bahamas, despite having given his word to the Queen. Other paparazzi, French, German and Italian photographers, were also heading that way, desperate for a bikini photograph of the Princess.

Prince Charles believed that he had total privacy on Windemere, and that any cameraman who did manage to get on to the island, which was only connected to the main island of Eleuthera by a narrow bridge, would be picked up by the local police. In the event he was wrong and he should have remembered that he was once photographed on that same beach frolicking in the surf with bikini-clad Amanda Knatchbull, granddaughter of Lord ("Dickie") Mountbatten, Prince Charles' honorary grandfather. He had once harboured hopes that the two would marry, but not even a paradise isle like Windemere could spark off a romance between the two who had known each other all their lives.

The sun was hot and welcoming on the morning of February 17 and the Prince and his cousin, Lord Romsey, were up early, racing from the cottage for a spot of water skiing. Diana and Penelope came out a little later, Diana modestly covered in an all-enveloping kaftan. At this stage of her pregnancy a bikini would hardly be right, would it? As far as the foursome could see the inviting white sands backed by coconut groves were theirs alone: a spot of paradise away from the pressures of their public world at home in Britain.

Four hundred yards away, four sweating, unshaven men crouched in the tangled undergrowth cursing their luck. The rivals from *The Sun* and *The Star* had teamed up in Nassau and flown to Windemere by private plane in advance of the Royal arrivals, to hide themselves in the bushes before local police blocked off the island.

It had been an uncomfortable 48 hours, hiding and swatting insects as they waited. Now their quarry was firmly fixed in the viewfinders, though still not good enough. Bikini pictures were what they were after.

Charles, the dutiful husband, put out a sun lounger near the water's edge for his wife to catch the best tan. The photographers just couldn't believe their luck for suddenly the Princess stood up, slipping off the turquoise kaftan to reveal a brief cerise bikini. The motor drives clicked in the bushes and soon those extraordinary revealing photographs of an obviously pregnant full-breasted Princess would be flashed round the world.

Wired by machine to London they appeared on the nation's breakfast tables. *"Stunning mum to be in the sun"* said the headline. Those editors without the sensational pictures sat back and waited for the wrath to come. They didn't have to wait long. Even more embarrassing were the pictures captured by one cameraman as another couple strolled on to that same beach. They were also on holiday on the tiny island and they too believed themselves to be alone. Charles and Diana, now rubbing sun tan oil into each other's shoulders could not see this other couple from where they lay, which was just as well. The newcomers stripped naked and ran together into the waves. They frolicked in the sea for some time unaware that the Heir to the British Throne and his wife were only a few yards away. Then the naked couple, still believing they had the place to themselves, went behind a nearby beach hut and made passionate love. This was seen by the cameraman, but fortunately for the Royal Couple the beach hut blocked their view. Finally the nude lovers left and the cameraman slipped away too.

The expected rumpus erupted quickly. The Queen issued a statement saying that the photographs were in the worst possible taste. A telephone call was made to the Windemere cottage and later the Palace said that the Royal Couple were "very upset." But in fact it was only Charles who was livid that his wife had been photographed in this way. Diana herself was not angry at all, only amused by the whole thing. "Why shouldn't they see me in a bikini," the Princess told friends on her return to London.

The early difficult part of pregnancy was over and Diana, now glowing with health and morning sickness a thing of the past, settled down to plan a most modern and unusual Royal birth. But before delivery day there would be drama, worry for her unborn child and one or two arguments with a doctor.

☆ ☆ ☆ ☆ ☆ ☆

THE BIRTH OF WILLIAM

THE PRINCESS paused on the top step of the long staircase. She was about to join the rest of the Royal Family for tea in one of the stately drawing rooms at Sandringham House in Norfolk. For a few terrible moments Diana stood poised on the brink of tragedy and could have lost the baby she was carrying. The crash she made when she lost her balance and plunged down the stairs that February afternoon brought servants and members of the Royal Family running from every part of the house. They found her in a crumpled heap at the bottom and carried her to her bedroom. Prince Charles telephoned for a local doctor, even although shocked, but unhurt, Diana had told him not to bother. The doctor checked that the unborn baby's heartbeat was still functioning normally and ordered the Princess to spend the rest of the afternoon in bed. Her own gynaecologist, Mr. Pinker, was summoned from London and after seeing his patient confirmed that there was no hint of trouble.

"She is a strong and healthy young woman. Any fall involving a pregnant woman can be dangerous but remember the baby is protected by the surrounding waters." The danger was over but for a few short hours it had been a worrying time, not only for the Prince and Princess but for the Queen too, who fussed round her daughter-in-law that afternoon, anxious about Diana and her unborn grandchild.

Fully recovered from her tumble, her child quite safe, the Princess began her plans to change the rules on Royal births and child rearing. Not for her, she decided, the anonymity of Royal parenthood with nannies doing all the nursery drudgery and parents just dropping in from time to time, or at bedtime, to see their offspring freshly scrubbed and neat and tidy.

Natural childbirth and a close parent child relationship was what the Princess had decided on. Even before the birth she told her astonished staff, "I've decided to take my baby on the first Royal Tour, I just couldn't bear to be parted." This, to many Buckingham Palace courtiers, was an outrageous idea...taking a baby on an official foreign tour – ridiculous! Diana persisted, and with her stubborn nature certainly won her spurs battling against red tape to keep her baby by her side. Even the Queen, by now getting used to the breath of fresh air her daughter-in-law had brought to the Palace, was amazed by this latest suggestion.

During the engagement she had grown amused by the sight of Lady Diana Spencer dancing her way down the palace's long carpeted corridors, a pair of stereo headphones clamped to her ears, oblivious to the presence of even her Monarch. Or to know that Diana was dancing in a leotard to trim her figure. But taking a baby abroad while doing official duties! The idea was out of the question.

The Princess would not budge. She had made up her mind and didn't want her baby brought up in the typically upper class way, taken care of by staff while she was wined and dined in some foreign embassy residence, secretly pining away for just one cuddle with her baby. Australia and New Zealand, the tour originally cancelled because of Diana's pregnancy, would be the first countries the Royal Couple would visit in 1983.

Although her staff all insisted that she would be ill advised to take her baby on such a long and arduous tour with more than 45,000 miles to travel, in the end the Princess had the final word and complex arrangements were made to accommodate her baby. The future Prince or Princess would travel on the plane to Australia, then stay at a secure home base with the nanny while mother and father went around the continent to meet their Commonwealth subjects. They would return to this home base whenever possible.

With that battle won, the Princess turned to fight on another front – natural childbirth. She wanted it together with a home delivery, and had no difficulty in persuading Charles to attend natural childbirth classes with her. They sat on cushions on the floor at Kensington Palace while a teacher from the Natural Childbirth Trust taught the Princess how to relax and breathe correctly, and how to use different breathing techniques to cope with labour pains. Charles was instructed in the ways he could offer help and support to his wife and encourage her during her labour.

He had already decided to be present at the birth, unlike his own father, Prince Philip, whose attitude was typical of his own generation. He had played a game of squash with his equerry, Michael Parker, while the Queen was in labour. At that time it was unthinkable for a husband to be present in the delivery room. Surgeon gynaecologist George Pinker was in full agreement with their wish for Charles to be in at the birth. "I think it helps the mother very much," was the advice Mr. Pinker gave to the Prince. "I also believe it strengthens family bonds." Mr. Pinker's caring attitude inspired total confidence. He was an old hand at Royal deliveries, and Princess Diana's baby was to be his eighth. But he was certainly not old fashioned in his approach. Mr. Pinker is just the sort of softly spoken doctor all women long to consult during pregnancy, and he was the youngest man ever to be appointed gynaecologist to the Queen when he got the job in 1973, replacing Sir John Peel.

He is a family man himself, married to a former State Registered Nurse, Dorothy, with a grown-up family of four, including twins. Despite his Royal clients, Mr. Pinker worked mainly for the National Health Service at clinics in St. Mary's Hospital in Paddington, and at the Samaritan Hospital for Women in London.

He had shown he could cope with a difficult crisis too in 1974 when there was a Royal baby drama. The Duchess of Gloucester, a lady who had lost a previous baby with a miscarriage, was rushed to St. Mary's, where after a four-hour battle, he won the fight for the life of a premature boy born by Caesarian section. The child is Alexander, Earl of Ulster, now a healthy 11-year-old. Mr. Pinker delivered both of Princess Anne's two children, Master Peter in 1977 and Miss Zara Phillips in May 1981. He was there for the birth of Princess Michael of Kent's two children, Lord Frederick Windsor in April 1979 and Lady Gabriella Windsor in April 1981, and for the births of the Duchess of Gloucester's two daughters, Lady Davina Windsor in November 1977 and Lady Rose Windsor in March 1980.

The capable Mr. Pinker has a stubborn side to his nature. He firmly believes that all babies should be born in hospital where there is immediate help should an emergency occur. Princess Anne, just like Diana, is a woman with a mind of her own and she had been determined that her babies should be born at home. After all, the Queen had given birth to all four of her children in Buckingham Palace in the Buhl Room which was equipped as a labour room for the event.

Mr. Pinker resisted Princess Anne, and it was he who won in the end and Anne who obeyed. This time too, when Diana tried to fight for a home delivery, the quietly-spoken, kindly Mr. Pinker won hands down. Diana gave in, just as Anne had done, because in the delivery ward Mr. George Pinker has always shown that he is firmly in charge.

Mr. Pinker had already made a booking for the Princess at St. Mary's in Paddington long before he had persuaded her that he knew best. The £126.90 a day room, just 12ft. x 12ft. with a view of the back of Paddington Railway Station, seemed an unfitting setting for the entrance of a future Heir to the Throne. The room was in the Lindo Wing of the National Health Hospital, and although it was used by private patients it was hardly in the luxury class. Harshly decorated in off white emulsion, the only concession to gaiety was a flowered wallpaper at the back of the wooden bedhead. But this room would be the focus of world attention on the night of June 21st, 1982.

A month before the predicted birthdate a jubilant Princess Diana found the perfect nanny: forest worker's daughter Barbara Barnes, then aged 39, unmarried and with no formal training, was given the job which made her the envy of nannies the world over. Attractive Miss Barnes was talent-spotted by Princess Margaret and recommended to Princess Diana. Princess Margaret was very impressed by Miss Barnes, who at that time was looking after the children of her lady in waiting, Lady Anne Tennant.

A lot of tears were shed in the Tennant household when Barbara finally said goodbye to the twins, May and Amy, aged 11. The children had come to look upon Miss Barnes as their big sister because she had been with them all their childhood. She was a tough, no-nonsense but kindly child manager, exactly the sort of person Diana was looking for to take charge of the nurseries at Kensington Palace and Highgrove.

The new Royal Nanny had learned her lessons on how to be diplomatic. Even before moving to Kensington Palace, while escorting her two Tennant charges home from school one day she refused to answer any questions, and when little Amy looked as if she was about to speak to a reporter Nanny Barnes whispered sharply from the corner of her mouth "don't talk," and the child obeyed instantly. The only condition Miss Barnes ever made to her employers was "I won't wear a uniform." This was not something that bothered Diana and she readily agreed.

Miss Barnes, dark haired and fashionably dressed, was a total departure from the old stiffly starched nannies who had brought up previous generations of Royal Princes and Princesses. Princess Diana wanted a more informal relationship with her chosen nanny, so it had to be someone she could relate to and Miss Barnes seemed the perfect choice.

Earlier, Prince Charles had suggested that they should re-employ his old nanny, Miss Mabel Anderson. Miss Anderson had entered his life when he was eight years old, and brought up Princess Anne and the Princes Andrew and Edward as well. Charles still adores Miss

Anderson who, after 32 years in Royal service, now lives in a grace and favour house in London. At 54 she was older than the person Diana had in mind and did not fit in with her modern outlook.

From the beginning Nanny Barnes was called simply Barbara. "I am not a graduate of any sort of college," Barbara told the Princess. "I have accumulated my knowledge from many years of personal experience." She was exactly what Diana wanted and their relationship over the past four years has been a complete success.

It's not often the Prince of Wales is tempted to shirk his official Royal duties, but the temptation must have been there on the weekend of June 19th and 20th in 1982 when he had to leave Diana's side to go off "nervous as a kitten" as he would later say, to France. He was taking part in the military ceremonies to mark the wartime allied landings in Normandy, but for the Prince, as he made a speech on a windy clifftop, the real battle was going on back home at Kensington Palace. Even as he spoke in France, he knew it was going to be touch and go as to whether he would make it back in time for the birth of his first child.

Charles desperately wanted to be there but the question was, would his first born wait for him? A Wessex helicopter of the Queen's Flight was standing by after the combined French and British military get-together had finished and he was flown back to Kensington Palace, arriving there at 4 p.m. on Sunday afternoon to be told "It's all right, nothing's happened yet."

Just 10 hours later, with the Princess's contractions becoming more frequent, the Royal Couple were rushed to a side entrance of St. Mary's Hospital. There were still several hours to go before the birth and Charles paced the floor while the waiting went on. And it was a wait, because the Princess insisted on natural child-birth: there would be no artificial inducements for her.

Outside the word was out. The 54-bed Lindo Wing of the hospital, in a back street beside the Western Region railway station had been turned into a fortress for the birth. Princess Diana's personal detective occupied a room just down the hall, and armed detectives from the Royalty and Diplomatic Protection Branch of New Scotland Yard patrolled the corridors. Dogs trained to sniff out explosives were in constant use and workers on nearby building sites were being carefully watched. Uniformed and plain clothes officers mingled with the growing number of onlookers and the huge contingent of Press photographers from all over the world who had set up camp across the road from Princess Diana's room. She could hear their raucous laughter as they set up their camera equipment to record the comings and goings. In the delivery room the Princess and her husband did just what the doctor ordered. At exactly 9.03 p.m. on the night of Monday 21st June, without much help from the kindly Mr. Pinker and his team, Princess Diana gave birth to a perfect, healthy 7lb. 1½oz. baby boy. Prince Charles held his wife's hand as she relaxed, exhausted from her 16-hour labour. Bursting with pride and joy they were able to touch their new-born son and Heir.

Charles, looking tired, left the hospital a few hours later to give his wife a chance to sleep. He was mobbed by a flag-waving patriotic crowd outside as he made his way to his car. His police bodyguard was engulfed by the enthusiasm of the well-wishers, who just wanted to shake the new father's hand. "I'm overwhelmed by it all," said the Prince.

Asked if his son was the prettiest in the world the Prince replied "Well, he's not bad." And with a red lipstick mark planted on his cheek by a well wisher, added, "He is in marvellous form. His hair is fair, blondish and he has blue eyes." And on the question of names he said, "We have thought of one or two, we have had a bit of an argument over them, but we'll find one eventually." Before setting off for Kensington Palace he appealed to the crowd to keep the noise down. "Sleep is badly needed in there," he said waving back at the closed curtains of his wife's room.

Back at Kensington Palace he telephoned the rest of his family with the news. The Queen was "absolutely delighted," the Queen Mother "overjoyed." Champagne corks popped both outside and in the Lindo Wing, and staff at Kensington Palace had a bottle waiting to wet the new baby's head the moment Prince Charles arrived home. The official announcement was posted on the gates of Buckingham Palace. It read: *Her Royal Highness the Princess of Wales was safely delivered of a son at 9.03 p.m. tonight. Her Royal Highness and child are both doing well.*

There was delight too from Diana's close friends. One of her ex flatmates, Anne Bolton said, "This is wonderful, exactly what Diana wanted. The baby must have come a bit early but she had it by natural childbirth and that is something she really intended to do." Garlands of flowers, enough to start a small shop, poured into the hospital. The Queen ensured that all her staff had a glass of champagne to toast the new Prince. The crowds both outside Buckingham Palace and the hospital sang "For she's a jolly good fellow," and the news was flashed to the aircraft carrier Invincible in the South Atlantic, where Prince Andrew was on duty.

The baby was the first child born to a Prince and Princess of Wales since 1905. He is First in Line to the Throne behind his father Prince

Charles, and pushes Andrew into third place. Being a boy deferred for another generation the difficult problem of sex discrimination.

If Diana's first baby had been a girl she could have been replaced as the Heir Apparent by any subsequent male child born to the Prince and Princess. The birth, just eleven months after the wedding was not the quickest in Royal history. Queen Victoria had her first child at the age of 21, only nine months after her marriage, and Queen Alexandra, as Princess of Wales, had her first, Albert, within 10 months of marrying when she was only 19. The Queen was 22 and had been married a year when Prince Charles was born.

As the nation celebrated, hundreds of Pressmen who had taken up camp outside the Lindo Wing prepared for action. It is normal practice for a mother to be looked after in hospital for about seven days following the birth of a first child, and that is what it was generally expected Diana would do. But she was anxious to get home, and Mr. Pinker had no objection to that. After all, Diana and the baby were perfectly well and could be taken care of just as easily at the Palace.

So with a nurse holding the baby and with Charles at her side, Diana, dressed in one of her comfortable maternity dresses, stepped outside to face a barrage of cameras. The couple took the baby home to Kensington Palace, and that was the last the world saw of the new Prince until the christening.

At this point there was a lull in events, for the new baby stayed nameless. No announcement came from Buckingham Palace, and the delay was such that bookies began taking odds over what he might be called. For behind the scenes a family wrangle was going on. It seems that like many other young couples, the Prince and Princess just couldn't agree on a choice of names. Charles favoured traditional Royal names like Albert, Henry, James, while Diana seemed keen on John after her much loved father, Earl Spencer. But the name John was associated with bad luck within the Royal Family. There had been Bad King John who had haunted them for centuries, and the youngest son of King George and Queen Mary was named John, and he was an epileptic who died at the early age of 13.

In the end the choice, announced on 28th June, surprised everyone: William, Arthur, Philip, Louis. He would be christened His Royal Highness Prince William of Wales in a ceremony in the music room at Buckingham Palace on the Queen Mother's 82nd birthday, August 4th, 1982, as a special tribute to the much-loved great grandmother.

Those who pledged themselves to guard Prince William's spiritual welfare crowded into the room where Prince Charles himself was christened thirty-three years before. The font had been made for the christening of Queen Victoria's eldest child, Princess Victoria, in 1840 and had been used to christen Royal Children ever since. Prince William's christening robe was a family heirloom made of fine cotton lace and lined with white satin. It had been worn by King Edward VII, King George VI, the Queen and Prince Charles at their baptisms.

The godparents were picked from a list of Royal favourites. Some were friends and some relations and they covered a very wide age group. One surprise was the exclusion of any of Princess Diana's closest friends, and another was that neither of Prince Charles' younger brothers had been chosen. Some names were not unexpected. They included Prince Charles' closest friends and those who had had great influence on his life.

First was the King of the Hellenes, better known as ex-King Constantine of Greece. Constantine, then aged 41, was a close friend of Charles as well as a relation. He is a cousin of the Duke of Edinburgh. Constantine fled his country nearly 15 years ago after an abortive counter coup against the ruling junta. For the last 18 years he has been one of Charles' most constant companions.

The second name, Lord Romsey, then 33, was no real surprise. He is Lord Mountbatten's grandson (hence the name Louis included in William's name) and he too was a close friend. The oldest godparent was Sir Laurens Van Der Post, then 75, a South African travel writer who has long been regarded as one of Charles' intellectual mentors.

The choice of the Duchess of Westminster for godmother was almost certainly made by Princess Diana. Five months before the birth of Prince William, Diana became godmother to three-month-old Lady Edwina Louise Grosvenor, second child of the Duke and Duchess of Westminster, one of Britain's richest families. The Princess and the Duchess had become close friends and, like the Princess, the Duchess was once a teacher in a London kindergarten.

From inside the ranks of the Royal Family, Princess Alexandra was named as another godmother and the last was Lady Susan Hussey, one of the Queen's ladies in waiting. Lady Susan played an important part in preparing the former Lady Diana Spencer for her new role as a Princess. The exclusion of Princess Diana's closest friend, her ex-flatmate Anne Bolton then 22, was a shock to friends of the Royal Couple who had been confidently predicting that Anne would be included in the list.

It was a wonderfully happy ceremony in Buckingham Palace Music Room, and Diana's father Earl Spencer commented, "William is a lovely name, it's a very old Spencer family name.

It was used for many generations, particularly in the Sixteenth Century when there were lots of sons around. I like it very much indeed." True to form, like any other baby, young William began to cry during the ceremony.

Afterwards, while pictures were being taken to record the historic event, Diana gave him her little finger to suck as a substitute for lunch as she cradled him in her arms. Every time she removed her finger the little Prince showed his irritation by starting to build up to a good public cry. And no one else's finger would do. Great granny the Queen Mother, and the Queen both offered theirs believing they knew from experience the quickest way to calm a baby. William was having none of that. Only mother would do and his cries started to grow louder. Members of the Royal Family put their heads together as the little Prince whimpered at the photographers. "He's got a good set of lungs," said the Queen Mother. "Yes, he is a good speech maker," said the Queen. Mother of two, Princess Anne, tried a few clucking noises of her own as Princess Diana blushed every time her son let out a yell, knowing that all he wanted was a feed.

Throughout all this noise and fuss there was one important man who kept well in the background. Grandad, Prince Philip.

Charles and Diana had kept the top layer of their wedding cake for the christening, and they asked for pieces of the cake to be distributed among 183 soldiers from the Welsh Guards and the Parachute Regiment who had been wounded in the Falklands.

Archbishop Dr. Robert Runcie took the 25 minute Church of England modern language service. He baptised the little Prince from the silver font which was garlanded with apricot roses and white freesias picked in Buckingham Palace gardens and the greenhouses at Windsor Castle.

The register was signed by the Queen, the Duke of Edinburgh, the Prince and Princess of Wales, the Queen Mother, Prince Edward, Princess Anne, Princess Alexandra and the other godparents. Two Royal signatures were missing. Prince Andrew was still in the Falklands, and Princess Margaret chose to stay on holiday in Italy missing both the christening and her mother's birthday. Queen Mary of the Hellenes, wife of godfather ex King Constantine signed, as did Princess Diana's father Earl Spencer, and her mother, Mrs. Shand Kydd. Last to sign were the Archbishop and his helper Canon Caesar.

When the formalities were over the Princess took her son to a private room to breastfeed him while the rest of the family and godparents tucked into a buffet lunch. Afterwards the Prince and Princess took little William back to their home at Kensington Palace and, with great style, the Princess asked her car driver to pause at the Palace gates while she proudly lifted up her infant son for the tourists and well-wishers to get a good look.

By Christmas, the next time Prince William was presented to the nation, he had really grown. Plump, happy and contented, the future Heir to the Throne gurgled and chuckled his way through his first festive broadcast clutching a plastic teething ring. And yes, mother had been absolutely right about the colour of William's hair. His Royal Highness Prince William Arthur Philip Louis is most certainly blond; he had masses of blond locks with not a curl in sight. A few weeks before the Princess had invited some Fleet Street cameramen into Kensington Palace so that the world could take a glimpse of William, and there had been some controversy over a suggestion that he was a redhead. Rumours gathered force when Princess Michael of Kent, a neighbour at Kensington Palace, told someone that she thought William (by now nicknamed "Wills" by his father) had inherited the Spencer family red hair. Princess Diana kept telling everyone "He's a blond" and of course, she was right.

The idea to let in the Press had been Princess Diana's own, after large numbers of the public, on the Princess's official engagements, kept asking "When can we see more pictures of Prince William?" Originally the baby Prince was to have made his debut during the Queen's Christmas TV appearance as part of a filmed intimate Royal Family portrait, but Diana persuaded the Monarch to let her grandson have his own Christmas photo session three days before hers. The Royal Couple, Diana in a Santa Claus scarlet velvet dress, sat on a plain sofa covered in pink silk and bounced the gurgling Prince on their knees.

The six month old Prince William was in a good mood. Nanny Barnes had dressed him in a white romper suit with blue embroidery. The Prince clutched a teething ring throughout the photo session, refusing to let it go. Charles and Diana, bursting with pride, played with him in turn, tickling his tummy and holding his hands. No teeth were on show, but the baby chewed on his plastic ring with vigour.

It was Prince William's first encounter with newspaper cameramen, and he reached out to grasp the hands of veteran Royal photographer Ron Bell. "What a grip," said Ron later. All his life the future King will have to get used to the all-seeing eye of the newspaper camera and over the next few years he would have further meetings with the Press, and turn out to be a real trouper. Prince William of Wales, everyone agreed, was a smasher!

☆　☆　☆　☆　☆　☆

ROYAL CHILDHOOD

PROTECTING WILLIAM FROM THE PRESS

FLUSHED WITH rage Princess Diana braked hard outside the main gate of Kensington Palace. She wound down the window of her black Ford Escort and screamed "leave him alone, alone do you hear, how would you like your children to be treated like that?" The Princess was reacting as a protective mother and the target of her wrath was a group of photographers clustered outside the Palace.

Prince William had been photographed in his pushchair being wheeled round the nearby public park by his nanny, and his mother strongly objected to what she considered was an outrageous intrusion. For the Press considered William's playtimes to be fair game, and the resulting prints were worth large sums of money to the freelance cameramen who gathered outside the Palace each day the Prince and Princess of Wales were in residence.

Throughout the ages, Royal parents have tried to protect their children from the curious eyes of the public, whilst still trying to instil in them the need to be brighter, cleverer and better than anyone else. It is hardly surprising that many of them grew up with severe emotional problems.

Charles and Diana are anxious to give their children as normal an upbringing as possible. That means letting them join the mainstream of life and meet and mingle with other children so that they do not feel "Royal" or too different. The Princess was annoyed because walks in the park were one part of this projected normality and it is hardly part of everyday life for an infant to be chased by four or five grown men firing off flash guns. The chastened photographers retreated. Little William's public outings were to be considered private – one more victory for the Princess.

Princess Diana had learned of the unhappy and miserable childhoods experienced by her husband's ancestors, like King Edward VII whose mother, Queen Victoria, made him begin an austere education at the age of seven, studying from 8 a.m. to 7 p.m. six days a week, and she wanted none of that for her offspring. She wanted no cosseting either.

As a child King George V was so spoiled by his mother, Queen Alexandra, that for years he would scream every time he had to be parted from his "mother dear," and when he grew up and joined the Navy he was bullied mercilessly by the other cadets, and always homesick. As a result he bullied his own children saying "My father was frightened of his mother, I was frightened of my father, and I am damn well going to see that my children are frightened of me."

They were shy, tongue-tied and totally unworldly as children. Queen Mary had little interest in her own, the ill-fated Edward VIII and his younger brother, George VI. She was content to leave their care to others. One sadistic nurse regularly twisted and punched young Edward and his parents did not find out for a long time. Another nurse utterly neglected the health of the future George VI.

It was not until the present Queen's father, George VI, had children of his own that life improved, Princess Elizabeth and Princess Margaret saw more of their parents than any previous generation. Of course, they never travelled with their parents, which is what Diana is insisting for her own family, and there were long lonely breaks as a result. But they did enjoy much more of a family life than their ancestors.

The really modern style breakthrough began with the public school education of Prince Charles, and the Queen ordered that her own children should never bow or curtsey before her as she had always done with her own parents, except on official or ceremonial occasions. But still the pressure of State work meant that Charles did not spend much time with his mother, and he was sent off to Gordonstoun school to be "toughened up" by Prince Philip. Charles did not fit in with the Gordonstoun environment and was both lonely and unhappy for much of the time he spent there.

Prince Charles and Princess Diana are determined to make childhood as happy and as ordinary as possible for their extraordinary children. So the battle with the photographers was just one stage of their joint plan for William and Harry.

The couple try to organise their lives so that they spend as much time as possible with the children. At Kensington Palace and at Highgrove 6 p.m. bathtime is very important. Charles dashes back whenever he can after public engagements to roll up his sleeves and help bath his sons before reading to them in front of the nursery fire.

At one time he became so wrapped up in the joys of fatherhood that he was criticised for neglecting his public work. He cut back on the number of engagements so that he could be with them and this earned him the wrath of Prince Philip, who is said to have given him a fatherly earful and told him he was not working hard enough.

He heeded this warning and picked up his workload, but that doesn't stop him getting deeply involved with the children.

In between public engagements – cutting many a ribbon launching a few ships, declaring things open and carrying out her charitable work – Diana, a Princess, who could have chosen never to change a nappy or empty a potty, takes part in these motherly tasks because she chooses to. The former kindergarten teacher loves babies, particularly her own, and spends almost as much time in the nursery as Nanny Barnes.

This then is the couple's blueprint for letting William and Harry be themselves, being brought up in as normal a loving happy family home as possible without spoiling them. Already the boys have developed their individual personalities as well as striking good looks. Harry, who has inherited the Spencer family red hair, (which Diana is not denying this time) is quieter than William, more relaxed and peaceful; in fact too peaceful, as Lord Snowdon found out when he tried to photograph the boys together.

The photographer was trying to capture brotherly love and recreate the photograph, taken in 1950, of the then toddler Prince Charles kissing his new-born sister, Anne. He even dressed William in the shirt his father wore for the 1950 session, and found a similar white satin pillow for the 20-day-old Prince Harry to lie on.

What happened showed the difference in the two temperaments. While William wouldn't sit still, all Prince Harry wanted to do was sleep. Snowdon was unable to capture an exact replica of the historic photograph, but the final result looked just as fine. Harry's naturally relaxed attitude is a complete contrast to the spirited William, who could sometimes be described as a bit of a naughty boy.

Mischevious is hardly the word for him ... his Just William style antics so far revealed include breaking many of his toys, forcing his parents to insist he be given only the plastic, unbreakable kind; making a mess of the Queen Mother's living room at Clarence House during an afternoon tea session; throwing his best toy spade into the River Dee in Scotland; attempting to flush his father's handmade shoes down a lavatory; stuffing hankies and toys down the same lavatory; chewing antiquarian books and smashing miniatures of Queen Victoria. In his father's words "he's so full of mischief he tends to break up everything in the house."

William calls Charles "Papa," which is exactly how Charles himself addressed his own father. Although both Princes have expensive clothes out of top-drawer establishments like the White House in Bond Street, most days they are dressed in hard-wearing dungarees, cotton shirts and shorts and woolly jumpers. They will both go to ordinary schools, and already Prince William spends two or three days a week with groups of ordinary three-year olds at a nursery school near Kensington Palace.

Later on, both of the boys seem set to spend a large chunk of their schooldays in Australia. Charles has already dropped huge hints about his sons following his Australian educational period because he himself loved his days "Down Under" so much. A family squabble might arise over plans to send the boys to boarding school, as Diana has already shown that she is not keen to be parted from her offspring for long. But the pressure from the rest of the boarding school educated Royals who believe it "toughened 'em up" will probably win here.

The Princes William and Harry are going to build their seaside memories on a shore that is forever England. The site for their Royal sandcastles isn't a white beach on some exclusive sub-tropical isle, or even a strip of Mediterranean paradise, but rather nearer the candy floss road to Bognor Pier. It's all part of the House of Windsor's plan to strive for a normal childhood, and the two Princes will be holidaying at one of three magnificently tasteless Spanish style villas near Bognor Regis on the South coast owned by Princess Diana's father Earl Spencer.

Charles and Diana are proving to be modern-thinking parents who have already broken with many traditions associated with bringing up Royal children. It is likely that the Princes will be joined by another baby in the nursery before long because Charles and Diana would love to have a daughter.

NEARLY A FULL TEAM

ON ST. VALENTINE'S DAY 1984 we learned the secret of the inner glow which dazzled and melted the cold Norwegians over the weekend of February 12 and 13. The Princess looked especially radiant and beautifully confident as she enjoyed a night at the ballet in Oslo on the Saturday. And she had every reason to be. Shortly before flying off to Norway on her first official tour without Prince Charles, gynaecologist George Pinker was able to confirm the news she had waited months to hear: she was expecting her second child and it would be born in late September.

There was time to pass on the wonderful news to Prince Charles, the Queen and Prince Philip and her own mother and father before the Andover of the Royal Flight took off for Oslo. Despite the obvious temptation to tell everyone in sight the Princess kept the secret through the 20 hours she spent in the sub-zero temperatures of the Norwegian capital. Her hosts, Crown Prince Harald and his wife, Princess Sonja, were kept in the dark about the pregnancy.

Prince Charles and Princess Diana have always made it plain that they intend to have a large family. She has mentioned the figure of four and he has dropped several large hints in public about more children. Just after their engagement they were asked what their first priority in marriage was. "Children of course," said the Princess.

Prince William was now 18 months old and it was obvious that the couple were desperate to have a second baby.

In September 1983 the Princess, believing she was pregnant, broke off her holiday in Scotland to travel to London to see Mr. Pinker. But the trip proved to be a false alarm, one of several she had endured since the summer of 1983.

Over the Christmas and into the New Year of 1984 Charles and Diana sneaked off to be alone together away from the rest of the family. Just after Boxing Day they drove off to Highgrove leaving William to go to Sandringham with his nanny. The couple spent four days and nights alone at Highgrove before rejoining the rest of the family. And then after the New Year they went off to the Swiss Alps, just the two of them, for more peace and quiet enjoying a 10-day skiing holiday.

The news was officially announced on a day meant for romance. The Palace made the statement at noon that the Princess of Wales was expecting baby number two. "They have no preference whether it is a boy or a girl," said the Palace spokesman. The news went round the world. In New York radio announcer Robert Harlan told his listeners, "The big story today is not Chernenko, not Lebanon, Princess Di is expecting her second baby."

This time there was not the problem of morning sickness. The Princess glowed with health throughout her second pregnancy and she made sure that none of her planned engagements was cancelled, even going to the lengths of taking helicopter rides. One big foreign tour had to be postponed, though, disappointing millions. The Prince and Princess put back their planned cultural tour of Italy for a year.

But although she was not suffering from morning sickness, this time her pregnancy was overshadowed by a personal crisis, a tragic death, which deeply grieved and bitterly upset Diana. For a brief few days it was feared that the shock to the Princess, then in the final month of pregnancy, could result in a premature birth.

On August 19, Princess Diana was in the nursery of Highgrove when a detective came in to break the news which made her burst into tears. Her favourite uncle, Lord Fermoy, had been found dead in the stables of his 700-acre estate, Eddington House, near Hungerford in Berkshire. Prince Charles, told about it while out playing polo, rushed home to be with his wife.

Police said later that Fermoy, 45, had shot himself through the heart with his hunting rifle and had left a suicide note. It was a terrible blow for Diana who was particularly fond of the man she called Uncle Edmund. His sister was Diana's mother, Mrs Frances Shand-Kydd. Prince Charles also knew and liked the fifth Baron

Fermoy; he had often stayed with Diana at Eddington House during their secret courtship days, using the estate as a much needed hideaway from the Press.

It was Lord Fermoy who made the famous statement assuring the world that Lady Diana Spencer was a virgin. "Lady Diana has never had a lover," he told spellbound journalists before the Royal Wedding.

The day after Lord Fermoy's death Charles and Diana unexpectedly continued with their personal plans for the holiday period. They flew with baby Prince William to Scotland and Balmoral Castle. Palace officials had expected her to cancel the trip because of the strain of her 36-weeks pregnancy, apart from the pressures of flying. At Aberdeen the Princess needed five minutes to compose herself before leaving the Andover of the Royal Flight. She looked sad and kept her head bowed. "She is very upset," said one of her detectives.

When details of Lord Fermoy's funeral were announced the Princess caused a further major upset inside the family by stating her determination to attend, even though the 1,000 mile round trip from Balmoral to Sandringham would be a long and extremely tiring journey for a woman so far advanced in pregnancy.

Many members of the Royal Family tried to persuade the Princess to stay in Scotland, but Diana flew down to Norfolk and back, even though she was very close to the limit after which civil airlines refuse to carry pregnant women.

It was a sad and lonely Diana who made the pilgrimage to Lord Fermoy's graveside in the parish church on the Royal Sandringham Estate on August 22. She wept as a lone trumpeter played the Last Post. During the sombre ceremony she leaned for support on the arm of her 21-year-old brother Charles, her head bowed, half-hidden by a black veil.

Prince Charles stayed behind in Scotland, although he did drive his wife to the airport to see her off. It was later explained that members of the Royal Family only ever attend funerals of close relatives or extremely close friends. It was a tragic time for the Princess, but neither the shock of her uncle's suicide or the long tiring plane journey affected her second baby.

The new arrival took everyone, including Diana and her gynaecologist, completely by surprise. He just wasn't expected so soon. Charles and Diana had planned to spend a quiet September weekend together at Windsor Castle. Mr. Pinker had confidently predicted the birth later in the week and had booked her into St. Mary's hospital the following weekend.

But in the early hours of Saturday, September 15, frantic phone calls were made from the Castle to Mr. Pinker's home. He in turn alerted his medical team as the Royal Couple were driven at high speed along the M4 towards London. Mr. Pinker was waiting for the Princess when she arrived at a side door of the hospital at the end of the 40-minute dash. Some hours later her new baby was born, 10 days early, just like Prince William.

Polo mad Charles, who was in at the birth again, and getting almost blasé about the whole business, left the hospital heading for Windsor Great Park to play a few chukkas of polo at Smith's Lawn saying: "I've nearly got a full team now."

The speed at which the young Prince was named Henry, Charles, Albert, David even before the Princess had left the hospital, sparked off speculation that Charles and Diana knew the sex of their baby in advance. There had been rumours throughout the pregnancy that they had found out following a scan and other tests. The rush to announce the names, just 16 hours after the birth, seemed to confirm those rumours.

He was Henry because there was no other such name in the present Royal Family. Charles obviously as a parental tribute to the father and because it is a family name on Diana's side among the Spencers. Albert after Queen Victoria's husband and King George the Sixth's christian name. The name Albert was also borne by Princess Diana's grandfather, and is Prince Andrew's second name. The David comes from Sir David Bowes Lyon, the Prince of Wales's great uncle. Diana is said to have wanted to include John after her own much-loved father, but the name, as it was explained before Prince William's christening, is an unlucky one for the Royals.

But the most surprising, and the one he will be known for the rest of his life, is almost a nickname. It was announced at 11.35 a.m. on September 16 through a gathering of Pressmen clustered outside St. Mary's. Mr Victor Chapman the Palace Press officer, approached them with the names and then added, almost as an afterthought: "He will be known by the family as Prince Harry." The crowds went wild about Harry, and their cheering was heard by Diana as she prepared to leave the hospital for Kensington Palace. There was no point in her staying longer than 24 hours, and it was much quieter back at the Palace.

Prince Harry's arrival was strictly a family affair, full of joy and laughter. William, brought by his father to see the new arrival, scampered along the hospital corridor to be swept up in his mother's arms before being introduced to his new brother. The entire branch of the Windsor family, proud mother, father and their two boys shut the door of their spartan 12ft by 12ft hospital room for 10 minutes alone together.

The Prince and Princess of Wales were carrying out to the letter the recommendation of every child expert on how to introduce the second baby to the first. And judging by Prince William's reaction as he left hospital hand in hand with his nanny Miss Barnes and waving delightedly at the crowds, that 10 minutes was a complete success.

With the Second in Line to the Throne safely back in his Kensington Palace nursery, Charles and Diana got on with the tradition of showing off a new-born Royal baby. Wrapped in a white shawl and cradled in his mother's arms, Henry, Charles, Albert, David of Wales, who will be simply known as Harry, was presented to the nation on the steps of the Lindo Wing. A crowd of several hundred packed into the narrow side street cheered and waved Union Jacks. A woman in the crowd shouted "Harry for England and St George," but it should have been Harry for the world because the touching event was seen by countless millions on television.

After the Royal Couple drove back to the palace, Harry still in his mother's arms in the back of Charles' Jaguar, nurses at St. Mary's told of the sound of laughter and giggling they had heard coming from the room on the fourth floor of the hospital when William met Harry. It was 9.40 a.m. when Prince Charles took William, resplendent in a pair of red shorts, a white shirt and white socks, to the hospital. Hand in hand father and son rode in the lift to the corridor where Diana was waiting for them.

As the doors opened William looked down the length of the corridor and spotted his mother standing in a dressing gown, beside the open door of her room. He gave a delighted cry and scampered down for a loving cuddle. "It was a marvellous heart-warming sight", said a member of the medical staff – and one which revealed what a completely modern Royal family Diana was raising.

Diana too was getting to be an old hand at births now. She sucked on an ice cube during her unassisted delivery, and even arranged her departure from the hospital between breast-feeding times.

And she was learning about dress sense after pregnancy. She made a mistake when she left St. Mary's following the birth of William wearing a spotted smock dress and a pair of extremely unflattering knee-length pop socks. But after Harry she certainly lived up to her reputation as an international cover girl by emerging in a cherry red coat over a red and white striped silk dress with a neat round collar and a fashionable bow at the neck. It was a right Royal choice for such an occasion and the Princess looked stunning.

Harry was christened in private on December 21 with the Queen carefully guarding the security of her own "exclusive" story. The Royal Proclamation was simple. No one, but no one outside of family and close friends was to witness the christening of the three month-old Prince. The Queen wanted to keep the story and pictures of the simple ceremony from the public gaze until Christmas Day.

A film of the christening, which was conducted as before by the Archbishop of Canterbury, Dr Robert Runcie, was seen for the first time by the nation and Commonwealth in the Queen's Christmas broadcast.

Press photographers and reporters were banned from the grounds of Windsor Castle as members of the Royal Family gathered in St George's Chapel. Even the godparents, Prince Andrew, Princess Margaret's daughter Lady Sarah Armstrong Jones, Lady Vestey, second wife of Dewhurst meat baron Lord Vestey, Carolyn Bartholomew, Diana's former flatmate and friend, Prince Charles' friend Gerald Ward and Royal portrait painter Bryan Organ, were sworn to secrecy over the day's events. It was the first time St. George's had been used for a Royal Christening. Apart from a BBC camera crew the only official photographer present was Lord Snowdon.

The Christmas Day film, watched by millions after their plum pudding and turkey, was one of the most entertaining Royal broadcasts ever. William poked his finger up his nose, ignored his father's calls, and pushed his cousin Zara.

Then, as if to prove that pomp and ceremony mean nothing when you are just two-and-a-half years old, he chased Zara round the legs of the Archbishop of Canterbury. The millions who watched were charmed and delighted by the warmth of family love at Windsor. And they learned why Diana always refers to William as her "mini tornado." The young Prince was shown squirming with impatience over his brother's big day. When his mother wanted to know if he was going to sing, the scallywag pulled a face and said "no." He ignored his father's call, racing along a corridor and shouting at the top of his voice. After the christening he crept up behind Princess Anne's daughter Zara and growled "Grr."

But the day was not without controversy. Princess Anne, who many expected to be picked as a godparent for young Harry, was not at the Castle for the ceremony. Instead she chose to carry out what she later described as a "long-standing engagement" to go rough shooting with husband Mark and other family friends in Gloucestershire. Her non-appearance was seen as a direct snub to Diana, a sort of a tit-for-tat for not being chosen as a godparent.

The speculation over whether Diana and Anne actually get on still simmers.

DIANA'S COURT

OF PERSONALITIES & BACKGROUNDS

SHE CALLS her courtiers Anne, Barbara, Evelyn, Alan, Paddy and Graham. They call her "Your Highness," occasionally Ma'am, and sometimes even Diana. In the court of Diana, Princess of Wales, democracy rules with an easy hand. But just in case familiarity should breed contempt, those who come to court at Highgrove and Kensington Palace know only too well that their mistress can be a formidable perfectionist who knows exactly what she wants from her staff. A girl used to making her own instant coffee in a crowded, shared flat is a very different sort of person from the usual round of Royals, born and brought up to pomp and privilege.

There are two courts around the young Princess, the inner and the outer: two distinct rings denoting levels of intimacy. These courtiers also fall into two categories...those who were picked for her, to guide and advise through the difficult path of adjustment to her role; and those Diana picked out for herself, people she instinctively liked, trusted and felt at ease with. They are a curious mixture of personalities and backgrounds – and not a member of the middle class among them! What this small intimate group shares is loyalty, trust and, most of all, discretion. They are picked with these qualities in mind, and sign declarations on the understanding that the gossip they are privy to, from the Royal bedroom, nursery or kitchen, goes no further.

The secrets shared by this coterie could make any one of them a small fortune. One former trusted servant of Prince Charles, his valet, Mr. Stephen Barry, who served in the Royal household for eleven years, has spilled all his accumulated upstairs downstairs tittle-tattle for millions of dollars for Americans to savour in paperback form. Royal courtiers are not well paid. One very important member does not even receive a salary, but what they do have is immense prestige and influence in their own spheres.

One other very unlikely close associate did come out of the woodwork to make money from a Sunday newspaper by revealing a few of Diana's secrets. After she became a Princess, Diana insisted on trying to continue as much of her previous anonymity as possible, even to the extent of driving from Kensington Palace to have her hair done at the same salon she had used as a bachelor girl.

This was a small establishment in Kensington called, appropriately as it turned out, Headlines. The shop was run by Mr. Kevin Shanley, then aged 29. He became so close to his client that she invited him to join her first Royal tour to Australia and New Zealand and later Canada, flying in the same aircraft.

He had a row with his Royal customer after she insisted on having her hair up in a more sophisticated style for the State Opening of Parliament...Kevin insisted it was a mistake and that it wouldn't suit her. In the end he was proved right, but their relationship was over. The rift between the Princess and her hairdresser had become too wide. The Princess picked Kevin's partner and friend, Richard Dalton, to do her hair instead, thereby sparking off yet another row, this time between the two men.

WISELY, Richard left Headlines to work for the Princess, and still does, and now counts Charles and the Princes William and Harry among his clients. Kevin spilled the beans about life under the Royal drier to a Sunday newspaper, and although he was paid an estimated £20,000 for the secrets Diana told him as he snipped away, his revelations were not exactly exciting.

Later, the repentant Mr. Shanley wrote a letter of apology to the Princess, mainly for telling the world that she was not a natural blonde. But one more little bit of normalcy and privacy had been lost to her forever.

In the case of tell-it-all Mr. Barry, the Princess is said to have been the person who took a dislike to her husband's valet and decided that he had to go. A more likely scenario is one of a new bride taking over in a trusted valet's hallowed area. Diana arrived, Mr. Barry left. Certainly he refused to say if he had had an argument with the Princess.

There are no shortage of applicants for Diana's court, but the Princess believes she has made the right choices. No one else so far has emerged to court publicity. Others have come and gone

though, amid rumours of clashes with a strong-willed Princess who knows what she wants and makes sure she gets it. Royal officials are always quick to dismiss any rumours of disharmony in the Palace but certainly it is these differences of opinion which have sent many who used to work for the bachelor Prince Charles packing.

One of Diana's closest chums is her lady-in-waiting, Miss Anne Beckwith-Smith. For nearly five years she has held down one of the toughest jobs at the Palace, taking on an immature teenager and guiding her through an emotional minefield and on to superstar status with dignity and style. Anne has successfully kept out of the limelight while pushing her young charge forward to maturity, and now as a result holds a job of immense prestige and influence in British high society.

Of course the job does have its perks – cruising the world on the Royal Yacht Britannia; staying in splendid palaces and residences throughout Europe with the finest foods and wines. Anne is the right woman in the right place, usually just a few feet behind Diana at official engagements. Of all her helpers, Diana is fondest of this sturdy loyal companion. The Princess calls her "Darling," rewards her with great affection, and everyone knows that they are close friends.

In the sometimes difficult atmosphere of Kensington Palace, Princess Diana has found in Anne the one person, apart from Prince Charles, she can rely on completely. Being a modern lady-in-waiting has its problems, as Anne will readily agree. It is a tough organisational role, and while she is not expected to sit gossiping with the young Princess over the embroidery, she must occasionally provide a confidential and sympathetic shoulder to cry on.

At 33, Anne is discreet and trustworthy, with an impeccable dress sense in the Sloane Ranger book of good taste – white jackets, blue jackets, silk gowns, for which she gets an allowance. She knows she must never upstage the Princess, and is careful not to do so. On Royal engagements she walks the necessary few yards behind carrying a large handbag said to contain emergency tights and make-up for her mistress. After nearly five years Anne is still full of enthusiasm about her role.

When the first Australian tour was over the Princess gave Anne an expensive pair of earrings with the words "I couldn't have done it without you." It was a graceful admission, and one that is very near the truth. Yet for all that devotion Miss Beckwith-Smith receives not one penny in salary, just the clothing allowance. That's devotion for you!

Another intimate of Princess Diana is Evelyn Dagley who holds the official title of Dresser to the Princess of Wales. She never makes public appearances, but since the day of the engagement she has been at Diana's side, sharing her secret fears, her happiness and her worries. In many ways Evelyn is a slightly mysterious figure who has been kept in the shadows. Promotion came suddenly when she was working at Buckingham Palace.

Evelyn, who is in her late twenties, was chosen to help when Diana was still a commoner, and they are now said to be extremely close. She would have soothed and encouraged as she fastened Diana's silk gown on her wedding day, sending her nervous young mistress out to face the nation amid a barrage of publicity no girl on such a day could ever have encountered before. Today Evelyn is in charge of Diana's enormous wardrobe, which includes countless kid court shoes (size 6½). This means travelling on foreign tours, carefully packing and unpacking and meticulously lining each layer of clothes in tissue paper.

Another confidante of the Princess is the nanny, Barbara Barnes. Diana, who picked Nanny Barnes herself, calls her "Barbara", and they hit it off together practically from the moment Princess Margaret suggested her for the job. Barbara, unmarried and aged 40-plus, had worked for 15 years as nanny to Lady Anne Tennant, looking after three of her five children. "She is exceptionally firm with a great sense of humour," said her former employer. "The children absolutely adore her."

Princess Diana is also close to two other burly men in her life: her two Scotland Yard policemen, Inspector Graham Smith and Sergeant Alan Peters. One or the other of the two minders, huge 6ft. 4in. Sergeant Peters or the smaller, handsome, dapper Inspector Smith, are with the Princess whenever she steps out on official engagements or just pops along to the shops.

They replaced her first policeman, Chief Inspector Paul Officer, Prince Charles' long serving faithful bodyguard, who Diana found "too bossy." Their unobtrusive manner suits the Princess, who even today had not really accepted the need to have an armed bodyguard a pace or two behind her wherever she goes. In private she calls them both by their christian names, and to others describes them as "my policemen." Both men have an easy, but not too familiar, relaxed relationship with the Princess whose life they guard.

Quite by chance, the Princess has acquired two most unusual and favourite courtiers. They are Paddy Whitehead, a Liverpudlian in his seventies, and his 65-year-old wife, Nesta. They were working for the Macmillan family when Charles bought his country home, Highgrove in

Gloucestershire: he liked them both and asked them to stay on. Diana, too, went for the down-to-earth outlook of Paddy and his wife, who the locals call Mrs. Paddy. She is the housekeeper at Highgrove and is reputed to cook a mean eggs bacon sausages and tomatoes for the rest of the servants who gather to eat in the big oak-lined kitchen, with its surprisingly old-fashioned solid fuel Aga stove. Paddy oversees everything on the estate from the cattle to the huge swimming pool. Paddy and Mrs. Paddy try hard to make Diana feel happy in what is essentially a family home.

Money is of little importance when it comes to serving Diana. What matters to those who surround this beautiful girl is that she be cocooned in warmth, loyalty and affection as she makes the great personal adjustments necessary for a commoner being groomed to be Queen.

ON FEBRUARY 25, 1981, Diana said goodbye to the only little piece of real freedom she had ever known. The day after the announcement of her engagement to Prince Charles she was driven across West London to return briefly to the three-bedroomed flat where she had spent many happy hours with the three young girls who were then her closest friends.

Number 60, a comfortable but not luxurious apartment on the first floor of Coleherne Court overlooking Old Brompton Road was the flat bought for her by her father, Earl Spencer, when she returned to Britain after a few weeks at a finishing school in Switzerland. Diana thoroughly enjoyed Coleherne Court which gave her a chance to spread her wings away from family and home ties for the first time in her life.

The girls picked to share this crowded flat, a brisk 15 minutes walk from all the delights of Sloane Ranger land in Knightsbridge and Sloane Street, rapidly became close friends. They shared each other's happiness and new interest over new boyfriends, and the tears and brief despair over shattered romantic dreams. Diana's flatmates, Virginia Pitman, Anne Bolton and Carolyn Pride, were among the first, apart from the Royal Family and Spencers, to know that the girl they jokingly called their "landlord" was to marry the Heir to the Throne.

Prince Charles never came to this flat, the Pressmen stationed outside 24 hours a day during the Royal Courtship saw to that. They made such meetings impossible. After Diana accepted the marriage proposal she knew that it must remain a closely guarded secret among just the Royals and her own family. But she couldn't resist telling her three friends, Virginia, Anne and Carolyn. What teenager (Diana was still 19) could keep such a secret to herself? The fact that none of them breathed a word during the three weeks up to official engagement day showed the great strength of friendship between all four girls. Any one of them could have made a fortune by selling the information to the papers, but they didn't.

Diana did it very quietly and with no fuss, just before she packed her bags to join her mother for a brief pre-engagement holiday in Australia. Anne Bolton remembered later that Diana walked into the kitchen and said simply "I'm engaged". The noise of Anne and Virginia's screams of delight were heard by nineteen-year-old Carolyn in the bathroom. And it was left to Diana to tell her flatmate the sensational news through the closed door.

"**W**E KNEW how much in love the two were," said Anne after the world was told the news. "But when she told us they were to be married it completely threw us. We started running all over the place, laughing and shouting. Diana just sat there giggling at our antics, clearly thrilled by it all."

The four girls, who had been friends since their schooldays, popped the cork on a bottle of champagne to celebrate. Even Diana, who in those days hardly ever drank, had some. None of the girls had met Prince Charles, but they were to be honoured guests at the St. Paul's wedding. The four made a pact that they would all attend each other's weddings, a pact that was kept. Despite all the security problems and publicity Princess Diana went to both Carolyn and Anne's weddings and receptions. Virginia is still unmarried but it is certain that Diana will be there on the big day.

The friendship of the three girls meant a lot to Diana, who was then an extremely unworldly and gauche teenager setting out into uncharted territory. Diana's second day as the future Princess of Wales must have been quite a shock to a teenager used to complete freedom. It must have given her a quick foretaste of the way the rest of her life would be mapped out both as Princess and one day Queen. On February 25 she woke in what was to be her new home for the first few weeks of the Royal Engagement, the spare bedroom in Clarence House.

Outside she could hear the sound of hob-nailed boots ringing on the cobblestones as a soldier wearing a bearskin helmet and scarlet jacket, his rifle sloped on his shoulder, pace backward and forward in front of the house's black wooden gates. On the other side of the house in a small green hut, was squad of uniformed Metropolitan policemen, guarding the Queen Mother. A uniformed footman brought Diana tea on a silver salver. This, to a teenager more used to getting up and making instant coffee for herself in the kitchen of Coleherne Court.

There were a few raised eyebrows among the Clarence House staff later as the Prince of Wales' lady brought a touch of teenage style to the Royal Household by coming down to breakfast with the Queen Mother in a pair of her favourite jeans and a sweater. Not that the eighty-year-old Queen Mother noticed; she was used to having teenagers around the house: Her grandchildren Viscount Linley and Lady Sarah Armstrong-Jones, Princess Margaret's children, often stayed at Clarence House.

Diana felt completely at ease in the company of her Royal breakfast companion, of course. The Queen Mother had been a frequent guest during Diana's childhood and had often watched her play with her other, younger grandchildren, Prince Andrew and Prince Edward. Another breakfast guest made it an even more relaxed atmosphere, Lady Ruth Fermoy, the Queen Mother's Lady in Waiting and Diana's grandmother.

Later that morning, accompanied, as she will be for the rest of her life by an armed policeman, Diana went back to her former place of freedom, Coleherne Court, for the last time. She had come to collect a few necessities. She stayed in number 60 only five minutes, emerging with a brown leather holdall before driving to Buckingham Palace for lunch with the Queen.

She would soon be known as Her Royal Highness and she would have to behave as one. For the rest of her life this quiet, non-snooty girl will have to cope with her every public smile being recorded, her clothes copied and her behaviour studied. From that day on her life would seldom be her own. She must have sensed something of the loneliness she would face under guard in palaces and stately homes because she asked her flatmates to keep in touch. Leaving them her new private Royal telephone number she begged: "For God's sake ring me up, I'm going to need you."

Diana attempted to remain on the close terms she had enjoyed with her former flatmates. They were invited up to the Palace and for long weekends at Balmoral in Scotland. Carolyn, particularly, helped Diana through the difficult period of adjustment to her Royal lifestyle in the weeks of the long honeymoon in Scotland.

But inevitably the friends began drifting apart. In time she will lose virtually all contact with her friends from those teenage years. The four girls are still in touch, but these days the meetings are fewer and fewer. Married life and more particularly the gulf of Monarchy, has split their former intimacy.

WHAT Diana desperately needed during those first few difficult months of adjusting to a Royal life was a new friend of her own age group, someone who was used to the grand surroundings and not at all impressed by the fact that her friend was a future Queen. When she first went to Buckingham Palace, to a suite of rooms there after moving from Clarence house midway through the Royal Engagement, Diana remarked how old those who worked and lived in the huge Palace looked. Her fiance was 12 years older and often away on official duties. She badly needed someone to talk to. It must have been a very lonely period, calling for a lot of adjustment from a young girl hardly out of school.

One June afternoon before the Royal Wedding Prince Charles took Diana to the Guards Polo Club in Windsor Great Park, a few minutes drive along private roads from the Castle. He was going to play a few chukkas, and of course a dutiful future bride was expected to sit and watch. Charles asked Major Ronnie Ferguson, his friend and long term polo manager, to find someone for Diana to sit with. Then the Prince went off to saddle up his ponies.

The Major introduced Diana to his young daughter Sarah, a freckle faced, bouncy, redhead, who has a natural knack of putting people at their ease. Diana and Sarah sat in what the Guards Club like to call their "Royal Box," a flimsy, wooden structure where the Queen often

sits to watch on hot summer afternoons.

Future Princess and keen horsewoman Sarah got on famously that afternoon. Sarah encouraged shy Diana to go for tea in the public section of the clubhouse and they were seen laughing and giggling together. This did not go unnoticed by Charles who, knowing some of the loneliness his future wife must be experiencing, suggested that Sarah should come and have tea with Diana at Buckingham Palace a few days later. The friendship, started over tea in June 1981, deepened. Now five years later, Sarah Ferguson is Diana's closest friend, and by playing a blatant and quite unashamed game of cupid, Princess Diana set out to ensure that her friend joined the Royal family, too.

In June 1985 Diana put Sarah's name forward among the guests for Royal Ascot week. Sarah came to stay for the race week as the Queen's guest at Windsor Castle, providing some welcome company for Diana – at least that is what everyone thought. In fact, Diana was playing her very deep game, hoping that Sarah, a girl with a keen sense of fun and an infectious personality, would catch the eye of her brother-in-law.

Prince Andrew, 25, the Royal with a deserved reputation of a man with an eye for the girls, was at a loose end. He didn't have any particular romance at that moment and neither, strangely enough, did Sarah. Diana made sure that her best friend sat next to Andrew in the Royal Box at the racecourse. The rest of the story is now part of history. The Prince and the red head fell in love, and announced their engagement nine months later.

Diana, of course, was delighted to have her best friend as part of the family. Sarah even moved into the suite of rooms at Buckingham Palace occupied by Diana in the months before her wedding day. Early in 1985, when the romance seemed to be flagging a little, perhaps because the Prince could not make up his mind to commit himself to popping the question, Diana, quite openly, began to push her best friend into the limelight, taking Sarah with her on official engagements involving Prince Andrew, knowing that the newspapers would seize on this sign of a future Royal Wedding. Diana's plan worked, the Prince proposed. Now Diana has a real friend in the Palace. Two young Princesses sharing a common friendship.

FIRST TOUR NERVES

IN A TOWN CALLED ALICE

ALICE SPRINGS, a tiny oasis smack in the empty red desert heart of their vast continent was where Australians took a first close look at their future Queen. It was a trip Diana had been dreading, her first foreign tour, and even before the Royal Australian Airforce Boeing 707 touched down on March 20, 1983, the mere thought of Alice was giving the new Princess of Wales tummy butterflies.

She had every right to be apprehensive about the start of this, the first of the many arduous foreign trips she will have to carry out, especially as it was Alice, with its image of the loud brash beer-swilling "ocker," a myth the Australians take a fiendish delight in perpetuating, which was her starting point. In a town like Alice, where they call a spade something worse than a shovel, the new Princess was nervous about a first Australian appraisal which would not pull any punches. It was an astonishingly long tour which lay ahead for this young novice, and when it was all over, more than 45,000 miles and six weeks later, Prince Charles, exhausted and wrung out by countless handshakes and acres of small talk

told his aides "never again, next time please make the tours shorter."

Strangely enough, against all Royal Household predictions, it was the worldy wise Prince and not his Princess who was shattered at the end of it all. The long tours' criss-crossing both the Australian continent and then the two islands of New Zealand proved the awakening of the sleeping Princess. She began the trip poised as nervously as a startled fawn, terrified to speak in case she said anything out of place. But by the end of April in Auckland, she had learned the art of making polite conversation to interminable notables at interminable dinner parties. She had shaken thousands of outstretched hands and accepted dozens of kisses. The first flush of embarrassment with which she had greeted the Australian sunshine had gone.

By the time the Royal Couple waved their goodbyes in New Zealand Princess Diana had passed through the fledgling stage to her emergence as a paid-up member of the British Royal Family. After being thrown in at the deep end in Alice, the Princess was ready for anything.

On the way she won a few million hearts, too, putting back the cause of Australian Republicanism by several years at least. Diana was an unexpected bonus, boosting the fading popularity of the Royal Family in this part of the Commonwealth.

The planning for that March 20 arrival had begun several months before when two members of Prince Charles' staff, his private secretary Edward Adeane (he resigned his influential job in 1985 over policy disagreements with the Prince) and his Press Secretary Victor Chapman, accompanied by a Scotland Yard protection officer, spent four weeks in Australia and New Zealand, pacing out every inch of the tour. They received make-believe bouquets, shook hands and stopped for polite chats, all with a stop-watch ticking away. The long hours of dedicated work were transferred to hundreds of sheets of closely typed foolscap paper which became the Royal homework. The Prince and Princess spent hours at Kensington Palace and Highgrove before their departure working out every day they would spend in public in Australia. No wonder Diana was nervous.

She also spent hours with her lady-in-waiting, Miss Anne Beckwith-Smith, and her dresser Evelyn Dagley, working out which clothes to take Down Under. The Princess's fashions were even then beginning to be an important part of her trademark and would come under close scrutiny from Aussie fashion writers, so naturally the Princess wanted to look her best. She was told she would have to cope with sudden temperature changes, from the searing heat of Alice to the rainy chill of Tasmania and Southern New Zealand. Everything from ballgowns, light summer frocks, warm wool dresses, even a couple of bikinis, were laid amongst layers of tissue paper in black trunks labelled HRH Princess of Wales.

There was an added problem on this tour which had never been encountered by Buckingham Palace before. Baby was making three and Nanny Barnes was filling cases marked Just "William" filled with an assortment of nappies, romper suits and favourite toys. A baby buggy and a sheepskin-covered car baby safety seat were also put into the hold for the 30-hour flight.

The plane, provided by the Australian Airforce, was equipped with bunks in a private forward section and there was a separate compartment for Miss Barnes, who was able to sleep in a first class seat alongside her charge, whose iron cot was bolted securely to the aircraft floor.

There was also one other member of the household who had never been taken on any previous Buckingham Palace organised tour, but he was considered vital over the next two months, the "by appointment" hairdresser Kevin Shanly. Mr Shanly would be the first person to see the Princess each morning after her husband. He was to play an important role in grooming Diana, the Princess the Australians would call "Beaut."

There were fears among Palace officials that William would not adapt to such a long journey. but he cried only twice as the jet droned on for 12,000 miles, and tucked into his baby food which had been prepared in London by Miss Barnes. An emotional slightly tearful Diana kissed her baby goodbye after the 7.54a.m. landing in Alice. He flew off to Woomargama, near Sydney, to live in a borrowed homestead while his parents got on with the business of meeting Australians.

Diana had to work hard to give the photographers what they wanted – the smile of a proud and happy young mother as her son was carried off by his nanny. It was the first time they had been parted and it was a very public event. Prince William, destined to a life of drawing the crowds, will be able to look at his scrapbook in future years and note with nostalgia that his first solo Royal Tour appearance drew only 25 onlookers and six Pressmen.

THE PRINCE and Princess joined their baby son every three or four days over the next month as they criss-crossed the continent from Perth to Brisbane. In all they boarded more than 50 planes during the tour, and most of the extra flights were arranged to reunite mother and child.

There was no chance of anyone tapping the Royal phone calls within Australia or overseas. Australian Telecom, still smarting over the world famous alleged listening-in to Charles' calls home to the former Lady Diana Spencer in 1980, imposed almost wartime security measures at Woomargama.

Round the clock guards watched the nearby Albury exchange; all workmen's access points on the line between the homestead and the exchange were locked and fitted with alarms, and the line patrolled 24 hours a day. Extra security measures for the homestead even included a ban on flights for a five mile radius around and 6,000 feet above. Members of the crack New South Wales Tactical Response Group, the equivalent of

Scotland Yard's Green Beret marksmen, patrolled the nearby bush, making sure that William slept undisturbed.

Meanwhile the Prince and Princess of Wales got on with the job, but even they gave away a few secrets in passing to the Alice Springs School of the Air, which has 110 pupils scattered over an area five times the size of Britain. The couple were questioned over the radio by some of the children who live in isolated farms, their disembodied voices frequently distorted by static. It was during the chat, also broadcast throughout Australia, that the Princess began to win the hearts of millions of listeners with her delightful uninhibited replies to the children's questions. It was her first real radio inquisition, she was obviously extremely nervous, but she coped brilliantly with Charles sitting at her side in the radio room.

She revealed that William wasn't crawling and had six teeth, trivia which was eagerly seized upon by the travelling international Press corps. To Jamie Smith of Ayers Rock she said "William loves his koala bear, but he hasn't got a favourite toy. He just likes something with a bit of noise, he's got a plastic whale that throws things out of the top, little balls." The ten-minute broadcast was filled with answers such as these, and the millions listening at home joined in Diana's laughter at the children's questions.

Although it was all light-hearted it marked an important step forward for Diana. For apart from a filmed interview on her engagement day, in which she gave a few hesitant answers, this was the first time she had spoken in public. It was good training for the public life to come.

Ten years before this particular tour Australian Royal reporting was still along the lines of "The Queen smiled radiantly and the rain failed to dampen the enthusiasm." But in 1983 the Press there discussed openly the most intimate details, even how Diana, a once well endowed busty girl had dramatically shrunk from a good size 12 to a small 10.

Australian reporters wrote about the effect on Diana's psyche, calling her a 21-year-old well-bred girl with a limited experience of life struggling from the effects of being rocketed from an unknown to Marilyn Monroe overnight. They said that the Princess looked as if she functioned more on instinct that intellect, sometimes confident, other times watchful and unsure. Worse for the young Princess, the Aussie fashion writers gave her a real dressing down, describing the clothes she wore for the Australian climate as "plain dowdy." One even commented "For such a lovely girl she dresses like a plain person who has figure problems to hide."

All this plain speaking came as a bit of a shock to Diana, not used to this sort of thing at home.

She was reading every word about herself in the Australian papers and magazines while carrying out long days of hard work; it must have been more than a little heartbreaking for her.

But in the end, despite all the criticism, Diana was a huge hit with Australians. Their feelings were summed up by one normally cynical journalist who wrote: "When the speeches are long forgotten and none of us can clearly remember when or why we were cold, hot or tired, the one thing we will never forget is the impact Princess Diana made on us. Was she worth waiting for, I asked in every city and town, at every school and airport. "Oh yes!" they sighed.

By the time Diana arrived in New Zealand on April 17 with Prince William in his Airforce cot once more, she was gaining confidence fast. She had coped magnificently with the crush of Australia and had brushed aside the criticism. She had even begun to stop hiding behind her blonde fringe and was learning to face the photographers squarely. Since her pre-engagement days she had a habit of putting her head down in a crowd or when faced with a battery of cameras. But in New Zealand the head was beginning to come up, the real Princess was emerging.

DIANA was really getting into her job. She kissed messy little faces, crouched down beside wheelchairs to catch whispered greetings, and listened patiently as teenagers stammered out a welcome. Without a second thought for her designer dresses as she crawled around floors in play school games and gave piggy back rides to a few of the luckiest infants. No one had ever seen a Princess behave like this before and they loved her for it.

In New Zealand she had even picked up enough courage to give a public ticking off to one journalist who had angered her by continually writing about how much he believed Diana was spending on her fashion. The Princess, her face flushed, berated the unfortunate reporter at a media reception saying "Why do you write these things, they are not true." She even had a go at him believing, wrongly as it happened, that he was the one who wrote about her wearing thermal underwear during cold official engagements in Britain. "How do you know this?" asked Diana. "Do you lie on the pavement and look up my skirt?" It was the international media group's first glimpse of the newly confident Princess, a lady who was not afraid of speaking her mind.

Much of Diana's confidence on that trip can be attributed to the nearness of her son. The experiment of taking William, who the New Zealand Press insisted on calling "Billy the Kid" was a complete success. The bonding between mother and child, which Diana considered vital, had not been broken and the Princess herself, struggling to cope with learning the tricks of the trade as a member of the world's top Royal Family, did not have to suffer from homesickness at the same time.

While the Princess was blossoming Prince Charles, an old hand at this sort of tour, was becoming surprised at the lack of female attention, and perhaps even a little sad at the thought of lost youth ... for a married Prince is not nearly as good a catch as a single one.

When he took his regular, almost ritual swim on Bondi beach in Sydney there wasn't a bronzed topless beauty in sight. Unlike years earlier when he swam from those same sands and he had to run for it when a nubile lady with the unlikely name of Bree Sommers pursued him wearing only a pair of brief salmon pink knickers and a thin transparent lace blouse which she later threw off to speed up the chase. In 1979 bikini girl Jane Priest threw her arms round his neck as he frolicked in the Australian surf. But in 1983 a married Prince didn't merit that sort of attention from amorous Australian girls. There were no fears as he gambolled in the waves, but all the same he was accompanied by an incredible party consisting of two lifeguards, one doctor, an assistant private secretary, a Scotland Yard bodyguard and assorted large men in trunks, the "anti beauty patrol."

The Prince kept looking around for the girls, but sadly not one bothered. And there was another blow to his ego to come...for he had not realised that the waves on Bondi Beach gave away a secret. The surf pushed aside his carefully combed cover-up to reveal that the bald crown of the Heir to the Throne was much more apparent. It was growing as his power to charm the girls waned. That was about the only time the Prince merited any attention in the Australian Press, for the spotlight was on Diana and William. They called the couple "Di and Will" ignoring that Charles was there too. It wasn't that the fiercely independent Australians had suddenly rediscovered an allegiance to the Throne, the opposite in fact because they believed that Monarchy is old hat, something to be enjoyed by elderly migrants recalling memories of home; it was just that the

people were in a mood to forget bush fires, floods, drought, inflation and recession and seeing in Diana a spot of escapism at the end of a long, hot and disastrous summer.

"Goodonyer Di" screamed the Sydney headlines when it was discovered that William was there because the Princess had put her foot down. The Aussies admire anything that smacks of a battle won against authority. "We like a girl with a bit of fire in her," they said. Diana won their hearts and her own Royal spurs.

In Auckland she showed off baby William to the Press, holding a photocall in a shaded garden, just in time for the last editions of Britain's morning papers. William gurgled with delight and crawled around, to the amusement of the cameramen, in a wonderful display of family affection and love. His first Royal Tour picture session was a huge success: in the next few years he too would become an old hand at posing for the camera.

Whenever Princess Diana moved through the Australian and New Zealand crowds, shaking hands and accepting bouquets there was one man who stood apart but was never more than 10 yards away. He carried a black bag with emergency medical supplies. Surgeon Commander Ian Jenkins hoped and prayed he would never have to rush forward. After weeks of constant travelling the doctor believed he knew the secret of Diana's success in Australia and New Zealand. I believe it is her tremendous stamina, he said. "While we all flake out she is still full of energy and just seems to go on and on. The mass welcome just fills her with energy." He himself admitted to being "absolutely shattered by all this travelling." Like most other members of the Royal Household he fell fast asleep in car convoys or aircraft after long days on hard pavements, but he said of the Princess, "She is amazing, she has no health worries on this trip."

The Princess had to draw on those supplies of energy only a few weeks later when, after a brief spell back home in Gloucestershire, she and Prince Charles set off on the road again to another major Commonwealth country, Canada. This time William stayed and Diana had to content herself with daily phone calls to Miss Barnes. She even missed William's first birthday, and a belated party was held at Kensington Palace after the Canadian tour was over. But Diana did not suffer much from homesickness this time. After Australia the Princess found she could cope with any foreign trips.

☆ ☆ ☆ ☆ ☆ ☆

MORE DALLAS
THAN PALACE

A ROYAL SOAP OPERA

DIANA'S FIRST visit to the land of opportunity turned into a monster soap opera publicity stunt with dollars and shameless snobbery the main objectives.

The visit to Washington and Palm Beach in the autumn of 1985 by the Prince and Princess of Wales almost turned the dignity of Monarchy into TV Hollywood farce. Their hosts for the incredibly flash five-day production were Ronald and Nancy Reagan, with guest appearances from Clint Eastwood, John Travolta and Neil Diamond. No good soap opera is complete without an uninvited superstar guest breathing a little scandal. On this occasion it was soap queen Joan Collins, North America's idea of Royalty.

This was a total departure from the ceremony which normally surrounds Royal Tours. The Royalty business was sold like some ghastly American commercial, and some observers suggested that the two stars of the Royal Show were turned into little more than performing seals. They smiled lovingly at each other and posed for photographs with those who had paid £20,000 a head for the privilege. The fact that it was all ostensibly for charity did not make the sight easier to bear. Diana wore glittering tiaras;

top British fashions graced her pencil-slim form. The perfect model's body, said the eager US fashion ladies drooling over her beauty and rushing to copy her gowns.

Charles made his usual wisecracks and posed action-man style on his polo pony. But apart from a brief visit by Diana to a drug addicton clinic, and a call by Charles on a slum rebuilding programme, there was little hint of the serious commitment to world problems that the Prince so often talks about. Charles never looked really happy on this tour, more like a man gritting his teeth and performing for what is known as a "picture opportunity," for these days Palace advisers seem to see everything in terms of TV or newspaper pictures.

Many of their appearances were behind closed doors, for America's preoccupation with security left the Royal Couple with no real chance of "pressing the flesh" of the real American public. There was virtually none of the beautifully unscripted and relaxed walkabouts which had charmed millions of Australians only two weeks earlier.

The couple's second tour of Australia has been its usual dignified success. They visited hospitals, schools and wandered the streets doing in public what both of them do best – being themselves and meeting and making friends.

Unfortunately Washington and incredibly rich Palm Beach was just Yankee Doodle Di, a social stamped around the future King and Queen. Those who lost out in the frenzy among the famous, wealthy and well-connected for the hottest ticket, an invitation to meet them, left town, shamefaced at their failure to mount the pinnacle of social success.

In Palm Beach, the most affluent community in the richest country on earth, those who hadn't managed to grab one of the £40,000 a pair tickets for dinner with Di and Charles came up with some incredible excuses to save their social faces. Agnes Ash of the Palm Beach *Daily News* said, "People who are not invited have suddenly found other things to do. They tell me 'I'm going on a cruise' or 'my husband is having a gall bladder out.' The excuses are endless. In Palm Beach you don't get miffed in public."

Charles and Diana are the world's most glamorous couple, and at the White House the Reagans pulled out all the stops to entertain them. This was the grand movie that neither Ron nor Nancy made in their Hollywood days, and the stars went to war for the Royal date.

The winners were Clint Eastwood – "It made my day" he said predictably. John Travolta – "What a dancer" he said of Diana after twirling her round in a fever on Saturday night. Neil Diamond – "I sang to her but I am so excited I've forgotten what the tune was." These were Diana's own White House dinner guest choices. Poor old Charles wasn't given any glamour queens of Hollywood to dance with and had to make polite conversation with the usual diplomats.

Joan Collins, the loser who didn't get invited to the ball managed to get into a Palm Beach dinner, upstaging Diana in the process and asking the Prince of Wales for a dance while his wife looked on. Charles was too much a gentleman to refuse and they danced the old-fashioned way round a charity event staged by the Prince's super-rich friend, Dr Armand Hammer. It should have been Diana's night but in the end it was Joan's.

Whatever the Americans might say about the Royal Family, their sometimes public view that it is an anachronism is just a pretence. Many of them would have killed to get near Diana, the jewel in the crown. The Prince and Princess of Wales are Britain's best ambassadors. It was a pity that their first taste of America together had to be dressed up like a Dynasty Special.

Diana may have enjoyed herself but it is doubtful if Charles did. His idea of a perfect Royal Tour was the trip the couple made to Italy earlier in the year.

This was the grand tour that Charles had always promised himself but never managed to find time for in his bachelor years. He obviously thoroughly enjoyed himself in endless churches, museums, art galleries and Roman ruins. Charles the opera lover and art fanatic was very much at home. He even brought along his own teacher to help him brush up on his watercolours.

It was supposed to be a classical education for Diana too, as she dutifully followed her husband round Florence, Venice, Rome and Milan. But she was not always looking as if she were enjoying herself. Sometimes, especially late in the afternoon in front of yet another statue, they looked exactly what they were: a husband approaching middle-age dragging a young, unwilling wife around all the culture when really all she wanted to do was to go shopping in those superb Florentine streets.

The British Press, unable to give their mass readership a daily dose of Italian history, turned the trip into a travelling fashion show instead. Fashionable Italy was always the place they expected Diana to dress to kill, but it did not turn out like that.

Before the tour began, newspapers were competing over how much the Princess had supposedly spent on a new wardrobe of British fashions to excite the Latin fashion lovers. £20,000, £50,000? A figure of £100,000 was, for the Princess, the final straw and she decided to leave many of her new outfits on board Britannia and turn out in tried and trusted clothes which had already been seen in Britain.

It won her nickname "Second Hand Di" but by this time the Princess had gained more poise and confidence and was able to shrug off the fashion writers' barbs. The Royals hate to look ostentatiously rich: there is little public display of their real wealth, and Charles has a reputation for not just being careful but positively mean at times over the housekeeping money. In reality what Diana spent on her clothes for Italy were nothing like the newspaper fantasy figures.

In the past, unkind comments about her clothes caused Diana a lot of distress, mainly because Royal protocol demands that she observe certain proprieties, like wearing a hat and stronger colours than she would prefer. Hats are inclined to make girls of her age look a bit matronly, but they are a "must" not only for the Royals but for people who line up for the prize handshake and who are politely requested (i.e. told) to wear one too.

In Italy it was as if Diana had said "I'm going to wear what I like and to hell with what anyone thinks." In Florence she wandered the streets looking for all the world like an Italian waiter in her Jasper Conran lightweight wool white jacket and black bow tie. But the Latin men loved the look and she won the heart of admirer Pier Luigi Peitini, who kissed her and handed her eleven red roses.

Even though the couple's long awaited gondola ride died a death in Venice in the rain the Princess dazzled Venetians with a wide-brimmed green felt hat straight out of Gilbert and Sullivan... a real "comic opera" said the British Press. Both outfits soon appeared in shops all over Europe and America, despite the expert criticism.

From the moment Lady Diana's engagement was announced in 1981 she became a fashion trendsetter. Well-bred, well-dressed, she was immediately dubbed "Super Sloane" in the influential Harper's and Queen Magazine. Hundreds of thousands of girls copied the Diana look worldwide. When Charles toured New Zealand before the wedding he was confronted by scores of Di lookalikes in white frilly blouses and black velvet chokers lining his walkabout routes.

When she became a Princess, with more money to spend, she had the time to experiment and achieved a wonderful often extraordinary sort of "prima donna" style. One brief public appearance in something completely different could start a rush. Shortly before the wedding she bought a pink Peruvian sweater in an Elizabeth Street shop in London's Knightsbridge called Inca. It cost just £11.50; the shop had 500 in stock – and they sold out in a matter of days. People queued to get their hands on one and those who missed out ordered the sweater in droves. Ever since it has been known as "Princess Di's sweater."

She wore a red machine-knitted sweater dotted with dozens of white woolly sheep to watch her husband play polo, and immediately British firms started churning out copies by the thousand.

Her taste for flat-heeled shoes, even if she only wears them to level down to her husband, became a lifesaver for the British shoe industry. Factories switched to making pumps, just like the Princess wears, and sold millions of pairs. Diana lent grace and style to a flat shoe which had gone completely out of fashion, and for a while every young girl seemed to be wearing them again.

It was no surprise to anyone that the Princess was awarded the title of Britain's Best Dressed Woman. She delighted everyone through the months of her pregnancy with a succession of fresh fun clothes. A few years ago the mere idea of a member of the Royal Family arriving in public seven months pregnant with an obvious bulge beneath a massive sweater would have been outrageous. But Diana's style has little to do with tradition.

Gasps of astonishment greeted the Princess as she strode confidently across the velvet lawns of Buckingham Palace in a beautiful peach silk dress and large white hat. But it wasn't what the future Queen had chosen that amazed guests gathered on the lawns for a garden party, but rather what she had deliberately not worn.

The Queen, Queen Mother and other ladies of the Royal Household were traditionally turned out in summer dresses, flowery hats, sensible shoes and seamless stockings. It was the stockings Diana had cast aside that hot June afternoon that caused so much talk among the British upper classes, wives of foreign diplomats and churchmen who had been invited to take tea at the Palace.

No one has ever seen the Queen Mother, let alone the Queen or even Princess Anne without stockings for such a formal occasion. It was part of the "uniform" their personal appearance kit for formal events.

Princess Diana's bare legs caused the tongues to wag, not just with criticism but admiration too. Because on that Summer's afternoon, with temperatures in the Nineties, her cool style was the envy of all the hot and bothered ladies who would have as much dared to go bare legged at the Palace as turn up without a hat. That is the secret of Diana's own personal style, the break with tradition, the sheer unpredictability which turned her into a one-woman revolution worldwide.

The boost she gave to the British fashion industry was comparable to the effect of a heart transplant on a deserving patient. Diana wears only British clothes, but despite the patriotism there is a touch of rebel in there, for in Italy she hinted during a cocktail party that she would have loved to be able to wear some Italian designer clothes too.

Only occasionally at big State occasions do we see a touch of those formal clothes which can add years to her age.

She started a trend in Highland gear after wearing a Scottish tartan outfit bought for £240 from young designer Caroline Charles. It included a little tam o' shanter, which is now spotted at outdoor events all over Europe.

Diana mania even reaches into holiday clothes. The sun-loving Princess popped into the Benetton shop in Chelsea for a couple of bikinis along with two pairs of halfmast pants – and started the designers turning out thousands of similar pants and bikinis at £30 each.

There was even a run on clutch bags when Diana turned up to an official function with one in the crook of her arm, so unlike the usual bag with a long strap favoured by other Princesses.

Diana is now recognised the world over as a poised First Lady of Fashion. The girlish frills of the early days have been replaced by an enviable elegance, and she carries herself as gracefully as a trained model. Her clothes have contributed to making her the world's top magazine cover girl, even after two children and five years of marriage.

Whatever she wears, a furry sweater or an exotic ballgown she manages to epitomise the contemporary look. That's Royal Style!

Clothing firms gasped along with the rest of us over Diana's almost total decolletage in that stunning strapless black taffeta number she wore for her first ever official evening engagement with Prince Charles. But since then they have been running up countless miles of black flounces. Everything Diana wears is noticed, admired – and invariably copied.

She has been a trendsetter in other ways, too. In Australia, after the Italian tour, she wore a fortune in diamonds, emeralds and gold on her forehead like an Indian squaw. "Good god, you're not going out like that?" an aide reported the Prince as saying when he saw his wife in Melbourne that evening. Diana did, and the world loved her for it. In reality Diana put the necklace round her forehead because the back of her neck was too tender from sunburn to take the weight. With those jewels on her forehead glittering in the light of a dozen chandeliers a slightly bemused Prince swung his beautiful bride round the dance floor as the band played a Stevie Wonder hit "Isn't She Lovely." And millions of women round the world copying the jewels-on-the-crown-look, could only agree. On another occasion she wore strands of pearls back to front to show off a backless dress – and started another new trend.

Their Italian tour wasn't frippery and fashion, far from it. Charles had tried to make his presence felt by attempting to bridge the ecumenical gap between the Church of England and the Church of Rome, but the event became a dismal failure.

Through his good friend and adviser Dr Robert Runcie, the Archbishop of Canterbury, the Prince had tried to engineer a mass with the Pope. The future head of the Anglican Church and the inheritor of the Throne of the heretic King Henry VIII asked the archbishop to make discreet approaches to the Pope to see if he would say public mass for him in St. Peter's Basilica. But the Pope suggested a compromise. Following the precedent set by the King of the Belgians and King Juan Carlos of Spain, both Catholic monarchs, he invited the Prince and Princess of Wales to an early morning mass with him in his private chapel.

Then extending the hand of friendship still further he asked them to breakfast with him afterwards. A delighted Prince Charles accepted readily, but his plans were foiled when the Queen heard of his daring ecumenical gesture. As head of the Anglican Church she promptly vetoed the idea, and six days before the tour of Italy began the Vatican received a letter from Buckingham Palace cancelling the arrangement for early morning mass, firmly saying that the audience would be enough. An angry Charles had to content himself with the private meeting with the Pope. It was a bitter blow for Charles who had been exchanging letters with Pope John Paul on the subject of world peace for years.

Charles first met the Pope during his pastoral visit to Britain in 1982 and the two struck up a friendship which has been further cemented during their long correspondence. There was a great sense of disappointment inside the Vatican that the mass did not take place, but at least the political wrangling took the pressure off the Princess's fashions; In all the ecumenical fuss the stunning black gown and veil she wore to meet the Pope went virtually unreported.

The couple's departure from Italy was a real family affair. Their tour had been a great success with thousands of Italians standing for hours just for a glimpse of them, and on May 5 Venetians finished their lunchtime spaghetti early and headed for the best show in town – the departure of the Royal Yacht Britannia.

The Venetians got an unexpected bonus, for as they surrounded the Britannia they were treated to a personal appearance of not only Charles and Diana but William and Harry too. The entire family walked on to the rear deck of the yacht moored in Venice Grand Lagoon, Prince Charles carrying two-and-a-half-year old William and Diana carrying seven month old Harry. It was an emotional public reunion with the children.

The treasure of Venice were forgotten and the beautiful St. Mark's Square was almost deserted as thousands cheered and applauded. Princess Diana looked close to tears after seeing the children again for the first time in more than two weeks. She was flushed with motherly pride as she cuddled Harry. The two boys had flown to Venice in an Andover of the Royal Flight accompanied by Nanny Barnes and two Scotland Yard detectives. They were met at the airport by Charles' acting private secretary, David Roycroft, and taken straight by motorboat to rejoin their parents on Britannia. Britannia slipped her moorings and sailed off into the Mediterranean, where the four of them could spend a private four-day holiday.

At the end of it, in Sardinia, two aircraft were waiting to take them home. Prince William does not normally travel in the same plane as his father for dynastic reasons, in case of an accident. He went with his nanny while Charles, Diana and Harry travelled separately.

☆ ☆ ☆ ☆ ☆ ☆

FUTURE KING
AND QUEEN

LIVING HAPPILY EVER AFTER

THE SIGHTS Charles and Diana sometimes saw on their way home late at night deeply upset them and made them think again about their dual role as King and Queen in waiting. After late nights at the opera or official functions, from the windows of their official car they saw youngsters ("hardly more than children" as Diana said later) some no older than 13 or 14 aimlessly roaming the streets of London under the yellow neon lights.

Charles wanted to see for himself how these children lived on the inner city streets. With just one or two of his bodyguards, and unannounced he toured trouble spots where youngsters sleep rough, talking to them and trying to find out what led them into living "under the arches."

What he saw and what he was told deeply troubled him and he discussed it with his friends Lord Tonypandy, former House of Commons Speaker George Thomas, who is a keen worker for the National Society for the Prevention of Cruelty to Children, and community architect Rod Hackney. He wanted to see for himself what was going on and came up, in what he described as "a quiet way," with a plan to alleviate the growing problem. He had kept a low profile, slipping away unspotted, fearing that if news of what he was doing were to come out he would be accused of dabbling in politics by either the Conservatives or the Opposition – and unfortunately that is exactly what happened.

Mr Hackney, who the Prince described as "a dear man but indiscreet" broke the Royal secret, leaving the Prince feeling that he was in the middle of a political minefield, looking as if he had been taking sides. Charles was particularly upset by Mr Hackney's assertion that the Prince used the words "When I become King" to describe how he would try to change Britain for the better. Charles insists he never made that remark, which he considered extremely pompous, and he felt that Mr Hackney's careless words had destroyed everything he had tried to achieve during those 18 months when he was out and about among the homeless.

Charles was keen to point out that he does not want to make this a political issue. As far as he is concerned the three major political parties, Conservatives included, are all working towards the same goal over the problem of inner city housing. The Prince had been meeting and talking with architects because he feels that people should work together to solve community problems and relieve inner city strife.

He would like to see troubled areas given cash and resources to help them eradicate the slums and rebuild. He believes a massive increase in community housing projects, homes designed and looked after by the residents themselves, holds the key to a better Britain. It gives people, reasons the Prince, a sense of pride and belonging. This idea has worked well in North American cities wrecked by the riots of the Seventies.

Charles has said that Britain is in danger of becoming a fourth rate nation, which means he thinks the country is a third rate one now. On this he often argues with his father. Prince Philip, who once urged British industry to "pull your finger out" in no way agrees with his son. He doesn't think the slide downhill from industrial giant has gone that far.

The Prince of Wales shares similar traits with the late Duke of Windsor, who as Prince of Wales earned widespread approval for his outspoken comments about the state of the poor when he visited the depressed areas of South Wales in 1936.

Edward, Prince of Wales, grew increasingly impatient with his life as a sort of roving "Ambassador Extraordinary" travelling the world representing the King on tours of the Empire. Charles too uses the word "Ambassador" for Britain to describe his role abroad. There were other similarities between the two men. Edward developed an obsession to escape from the world of publicity and State affairs, disappearing to Fort Belvedere, a castellated semi-folly near Sunningdale which he modernised and where he developed an interest in gardening. Highgrove is Prince Charles' Fort Belvedere and there is a theory that he too may be suffering from the effects of being a King-in-waiting, although things are a little different these days. Edward was never shown the contents of dispatch boxes because his father displayed no confidence in him. This is not the case with Charles, who has been trained as future Head of State since childhood.

When Charles was about to graduate from Cambridge he was given a booklet called *"Choosing a Career."* His fellow students may have found it useful, but he had no need of it. The Prince's future has never been in doubt, and he has been prepared for his destiny. He is almost ready to be King and more than competent to cope with the responsibilities of Monarchy. This future King has been carefully groomed for the part, but unlike an actor he does not know when he will have to go on stage to play the role. The date of the Opening Night is still unknown.

The Throne did not come to Queen Victoria's eldest son, Edward, Prince of Wales, until he was sixty. He became bored with waiting and turned to a dissolute life among shady friends and mistresses. Whilst Charles does not show any of the basic character defects of Edward VII it would be a pity, some argue, if he had to hang around too long before his Coronation.

Happily, the Queen is still a healthy woman, satisfied with her job and as deeply interested as ever in the Affairs of State. So Charles will pass more years as Prince than as King. The longevity of the females of the houses of Saxe-Coburg-Gotha and Windsor is formidable. Queen Victoria lived to be eighty-one, Queen Mary eighty-five. The present Queen Mother is as old as the century and still going strong. The Prince of Wales, twenty-two years younger than his mother, must expect, and hope, that she will live at least as long.

Charles has dismissed suggestions that his mother should soon give up the Throne in his favour. He says, in public anyway, he sees no reason why she should retire. He feels that because of the vast constitutional and political knowledge a Monarch acquires by the time he or she reaches normal retirement age, the Sovereign is then at his or her "most useful stage."

It could be the beginning of the Twenty-First century before Charles reaches the Throne. When he takes it, with Queen Diana alongside him, it will more than likely be as King Charles III. But if he wishes he could choose another name, for a monarch is not restricted to the names with which he was baptised. Even if he sticks to his four christian names he could also be known as King Philip, King Arthur or King George VII.

A youthful King and Queen would be very popular, both at home and abroad. The Queen was only twenty-six when she came to the Throne and there were many hopes of a new, expanding Elizabethan Age for Britain. For many reasons that feeling of national renaissance slowly died away amid a shattered economy and disintegrating colonial outposts. Could two young leaders like Charles and Diana put vitality and purpose back into Britain again? Rekindle the spirit that began with the Falkland War and provide a new unifying force for the Commonwealth?

The British Monarchy has been forced to keep in step with developments in the streets outside palaces and castles, and Charles revealed his awareness of the new society when he said "In these times the Monarchy is called into question, it is not taken for granted as it used to be. In that sense one has to be far more professional, I think, than one ever used to be." Of the task ahead he said: "I've been trained to do it and I feel part of the job. I have this feeling of duty towards Britain, towards the United Kingdom and the Commonwealth. I feel there is a great deal I can do if I am given the chance to do it."

Princess Diana is already out on those streets contributing to a future Britain. She is concentrating her work among the dying in hospices, addicts at clinics trying to beat the habit, even women sheltering in safe houses after being beaten by their husbands. When her public role began she mingled mainly with children in nurseries and schools. That was only natural for a former kindergarten helper. But now her work has matured; she doesn't want to spend her time planting trees and opening or closing organised events. She is trying to make a worthwhile contribution to life in Britain.

THE HARROWING visit to the dying (she came back in tears after a young woman told her "I want to live long enough to see the flowers of spring") will help her to prepare for difficult visits to Commonwealth countries like India, Bangladesh and West Africa, where she will almost certainly be faced with poverty and despair in the raw. Even the shocking sight of a diseased, dying child must not reduce a Princess to tears in public. The hospices are steeling Diana for that future so that it will not come as much of a shock.

In the wards she chats to the sick who have no hope... about this, about that, small talk but never condescending... about embroidery, a possible bet that day at Ascot, even television soap operas, and makes everyone feel that she really is interested in what she is being told, trivia or not.

In this aspect of her personality she shares many of the finer points which have made the 86-year-old Queen Mother into a much loved and revered Royal. They both have the common touch, people feel they can identify with them. Even in the largest crowd the Queen Mother can make her presence felt, and so now can Diana. They have the special knack of seeming to look into every single face and give a special personal smile to each person. In any hospital after a

Diana visit patients will say; "She really was interested in us, not like some women who come to speak to you as a duty. We can tell the difference."

Diana has the astonishing gift of being sincerely interested, no matter how dull or boring the occasion. Like the Queen Mother she radiates such goodwill and good behaviour that no ill-will or bad feelings could flourish in such an atmosphere. Diana spent the night before the Royal Wedding at Clarence House, chatting to the Queen Mother and watching a display of Royal celebratory fireworks on television. The Queen Mother had known Diana since her childhood and must have been delighted when her favourite grandson announced his engagement to her.

The former Lady Diana Spencer is now a fully fledged member of what Charles' grandfather George VI called "The Family Firm." They will take the Throne at a time of changing attitudes towards monarchies. Already Charles realises that the days of the aloof king on a golden throne are over and that the continuation of his own inheritance is being questioned in the Houses of Parliament.

With this in mind Charles and Diana are trying, probably harder than any of their predecessors, to get closer to the people they will one day rule. The brief tour of Washington and Palm Beach was a lesson warning them against being dragged down to the soap opera level of Dallas and Dynasty.

Charles once admitted he had no idea how people existed in small houses or rented flats, or how they coped on meagre salaries. His understanding is growing because constantly he has sought to meet as many people as possible from all walks of life to discover their hopes, their ambitions. Charles says frankly: "I'm not a normal person in the sense that I was born to be King. I could never be a normal person because I have been prepared to reign over my subjects."

Princess Diana is now learning the same lessons. Their popularity at home and abroad shows that they are succeeding in breaking down the barriers between Palace and People. After five years they are living happily ever after.

The Prince and Princess of Wales leave St. Mary's Hospital, Paddington, in June 1982 with their new-born baby, Prince William, second in the line of succession to the Throne. As these pictures show, Prince Charles had become a doting father overnight.

The first official pictures of Prince William with his parents were taken by Lord Snowdon at Kensington Palace in July 1982, one month after his birth. The young Prince obligingly stayed awake for his first photo-call.

Princess Diana poses with her baby, Prince William (left) for this most important first picture session – pictures the whole world were clamouring to see. (Above) Prince Charles is seen here carrying his son in a Moses basket down the steps of a Royal flight when arriving at Aberdeen Airport in August 1982 for a prolonged holiday at Balmoral Castle.

Prince William was fast becoming a veteran of the air when in March 1983 he accompanied his parents on the long flight that began their tour of Australia and New Zealand. These pictures show the young Prince William being carried by Nanny Barnes to the aircraft, closely followed by an armed Royal detective. The following day Prince William showed no signs of tiredness (right) as he landed with his parents at Alice Springs in Australia.

An enthusiastic welcome awaited the Prince and Princess of Wales when they visited the School of the Air, the education-by-wireless service which gives daily schooling to children living in the remotest corners of the Northern Territory. This was followed by a visit to Ayres Rock, which is the largest monolith in the world and is situated south of Lake Amadeus. The Royal Couple toured this massive feature, which dominates the flat scrubby landscape, on a blazing hot afternoon. They even climbed part of the rock.

The outfit that caused a sensation in Australia and stunned the world was worn by Princess Diana (for the first and only time) in Adelaide on April 5th 1983 when the Royal couple visited the school children of the Memorial Oval at Port Pirie.

The trip to Australia would never
have been complete without an
evening out (left) at the State
Reception. This was held at the
Wrest Point Hotel, Hobart,
Tasmania in March 1983. Diana
wore the Spencer Family tiara. In
Sydney, the Royal couple attended a
ball at the Wentworth Hotel. It
wasn't long before they took to the
dance floor (overleaf).

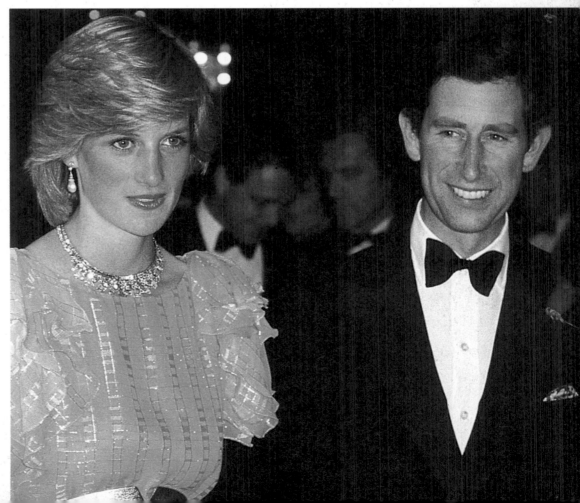

Prince Edward was on hand to welcome his brother and sister-in-law at Wanganui, New Zealand. He had taken a temporary post as Housemaster of Wanganui Collegiate. Prince Charles and Princess Diana were greatly amused by the Maori cloak worn by Prince Edward (and overleaf).

Princess Diana met the Maori Nation for the first time on a visit to a stadium in Auckland on 18th April 1983. She was very impressed with the traditional Maori challenge. The Princess, wearing garlands presented to her when she arrived at the stadium, later had time for a walk-about with Prince Charles and also an opportunity to speak to some of the children.

Princess Diana met the Maoris once more when visiting the Bay of Islands in April 1983. Both Prince Charles and Princess Diana were taken on a trip in a traditional Maori canoe, called a Nga Toko Matawhaorua (above and overleaf).

Prince William officially met the Press of Australia on the lawns of Government House in Wellington (above and in the following pages). He was not the least interested in all the attention: he crawled, turned up the rug, showed his seven precious teeth, bit his bright wooden toy bee and took a few steps, almost unaided. His parents looked proudly on.

It was back to the Klondike style of 1896 when Prince Charles and Princess Diana visited the Edmonton Historical Monument, where they attended a barbecue. Princess Diana wore a pink silk and cream day dress, while Prince Charles selected a suit modelled from one his Great-Great-Grandfather would have worn and who, as Prince of Wales, visited the goldfields at the turn of the century (and next four pages).

Back in England, Prince Charles and Princess Diana attended Ascot week. The Princess took full advantage of the opportunity to show off her new fashions. Diana is seen here (left) escorting Her Majesty, Queen Elizabeth The Queen Mother, in the traditional coach procession from Windsor Castle to the racecourse.

Sunday afternoons at Smith's Lawn, Windsor Great Park, is where the Royals gather to watch or play polo. Diana is an avid fan and loves watching whether her husband is playing or not. Left, Princess Diana and Lady Sarah Armstrong-Jones discuss the game and (above) The Prince and Princess of Wales applaud the winning team.

Prince William attended his first photo-call with the British Press in the gardens of Kensington Palace in December 1983. Warmly wrapped against the cold and carefully watched by his parents, the young prince was enthralled by all the activity around him and especially with the aeroplanes flying frequently overhead (above and overleaf).

Prince Charles has taken his wife on two ski-ing holidays – to Cadiz in Liechtenstein in January 1984 and January 1985, preferring Cadiz to the small chalet he used to rent at Klosters in Switzerland. Both Prince Charles and Princess Diana are expert skiers, the Princess having learned while at finishing school in Switzerland. However, Diana did need a quick re-cap (overleaf) before setting off down the slopes.

On the occasion of his second birthday in May 1984, Prince William once again entertained the Press in the gardens of Kensington Palace. He was turning out to be an inquisitive little boy, fascinated by the battery of cameras that faced him, and keen to investigate.

Prince Charles bought a football especially for his son's birthday photocall, but Prince William was not interested in the least – perhaps he will turn out to be a rugby player like his Uncle Edward!

With Daddy to lend a hand, a ride on the swing seemed a marvellous idea. Much more fun than kicking a football!

Princess Diana, a mother for the second time, leaves St. Mary's Hospital, Paddington, escorted by Prince Charles following the birth of Prince Henry in September 1984. The Princess left the hospital 24 hours after giving birth.

The balcony of Buckingham Palace is full of young children these days. Here, they excitedly await the fly-past by the Royal Air Force after the Trooping the Colour ceremony.

Prince Henry was supposed to be the star at his christening but Prince William was determined to steal the show. The godparents were Lady Sarah Armstrong-Jones, artist Bryan Organ, Gerald Ward (standing left), Carolyn Bartholomew and Lady Susan Hussey (standing right).

The proud mother and father
with Prince Henry after his
christening at Buckingham
Palace. Princess Diana and Her
Majesty, Queen Elizabeth The
Queen Mother take turns
holding Prince Henry.

For a brief visit to the town of Livorno, Princess Diana surprised and delighted her Italian fashion critics with a "slim Jim" tie and cutaway collar similar to those worn by British rock stars in the 1960's. Complemented by a white silk blouse and Jasper Conran emerald green wool suit, the Royal outfit soon appeared for sale in many thousands of fashion houses. During a visit to the Commonwealth war graves cemetery at Anzio, near Rome, fashion interest moved from Diana to Charles, who strode out for this ceremony in full Scottish Highland regalia completely upstaging Diana's maroon striped satin dress with mutton-styled sleeves.

All Italy was waiting to see what Diana would wear for a night at the opera in Milan. But despite rumours of a wonderful new creation for the glittering occasion, Diana wore a very simple pink evening dress of chiffon with a drop waist and tie shoulder straps. Her choice, made possibly because of criticism in Britain over the housekeeping she was said to have spent on her clothes for Italy, disappointed Italian fashion writers. But the audience who turned up at La Scala for a performance of Puccini's opera 'Turandot' were not disappointed; they applauded her stunning but simple choice.

Princess Diana putting on the glamour at a reception in Florence. This time she is wearing a glittering cocktail dress designed by Jacques Azagury. The black velvet bead-spangled bodice complements the ink-blue organza frilled skirt.

This is the moment Diana was dreading…her first meeting with Pope John Paul II, knowing that the eyes of the world were on her. The dress Diana chose for this historic meeting, in stunning black lace with full black mantilla headdress and veil, by unknown London designer Catherine Walker, was perfect. The Princess created the right mood of sombre presence rather than penitence. Diana went into the private Vatican meeting feeling "terrified". She came out all smiles, all her worries and fears smoothed over by a wonderfully diplomatic Pope. The brief private audience hid a Royal drama. Prince Charles had planned to take communion with Pope John Paul, only to have his plans for Anglican and Catholic togetherness ruined by the direct intervention of the Queen. The Prince and the Polish Pope have been, and still are, regularly in private correspondence over the problems of the two Churches. (And the next five pages)

Prince Charles and Princess Diana arrive in La Speiza, the naval dockyard. Appropriately, Princess Diana wore a

Beautifully-cut coat dress with a nautical flavour of pale cream with navy stripe, topped off with a small sailor style hat.

This is the astonishing outfit Diana chose to end her grand Italian tour, a fashion extravaganza which some British commentators called a real Royal comic opera straight out of Gilbert and Sullivan. She wore it for her Venice gondola ride – a green and black baggy coat with large padded shoulders and a large flat brimmed felt hat straight out of the 1940s. The outfit was designed by the Emmanuels, the couple who made the much-criticised Royal wedding dress. (and overleaf) Diana was still wearing the same outfit later that day when, in a wonderfully warm scene of family love, she welcomed her sons William and Harry on board the Royal Yacht Britannia in the Venice Grand lagoon.

The weather was far from good when The Prince and Princess of Wales visited Barra, in the Western Isles. But the cold and rain didn't dampen the smiles all around as Prince Charles and Princess Diana posed on the quayside with lobster pots, and later with some of the Islanders (overleaf).

Winning a polo match has two distinct rewards for Prince Charles: first, he receives a trophy to add to the dozens he already possesses, and secondly, since the trophies are often presented by Princess Diana, he is rewarded with a kiss. Overleaf, Prince Charles in action during a polo match at Smith's Lawn, Windsor Great Park.

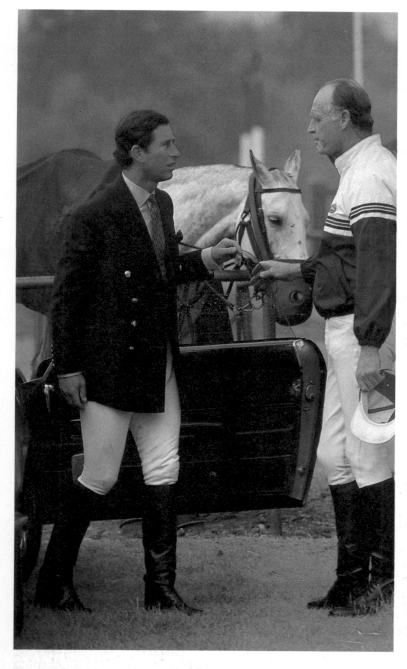

Prince Charles (left) discusses tactics with his polo manager, Major Ron Ferguson, who has been a close friend for many years, while Princess Diana enjoys the company of Major Ferguson's daughter, Sarah, Prince Andrew's fiancée. Soon the two friends will be sisters-in-law.

Holidays at Balmoral Castle – and the Royal Family attends the Braemar Games…the Scottish Mini-Olympics. It is a time to enjoy the show and joke with the competitors. For Charles and Diana, it is also time to show their love for one another, to the delight of the massive crowds (overleaf).

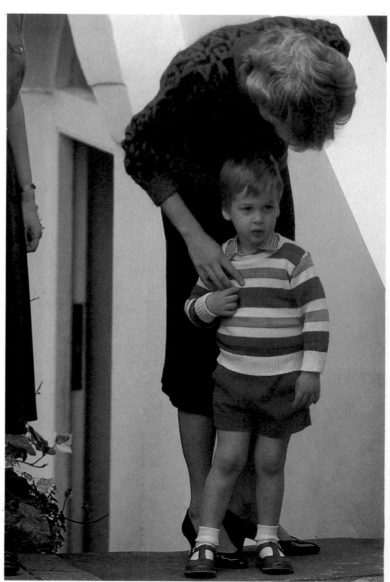

September 1985 was an important date for Prince William. He attended his first day at school and, like millions of other parents, the Prince and Princess of Wales accompanied their three-year-old son to his new nursery school in West London.

The classroom where Prince William will study and play at his nursery school, under the supervision of teacher Mrs Mynors.

Princess Diana loves all children and they love her. When she visited a playgroup in Melbourne, Australia (top left) she quickly made friends with the toddlers and one especially, who took her hand.

There was a special smile from Princess Diana for the children of Macedon (above and left), a town that was destroyed by bush fires. (Right) A tender look for Prince Charles in Canberra, and fun and games when Princess Diana joined in the driving of small cars for a children's road safety training programme.

This is the Indian squaw look which made Prince Charles gasp with astonishment the night before he took Princess Diana to a ball in Melbourne, Australia. "You're not going out like that?" asked the Prince. "Yes!" said Diana, and the world loved her for it. She danced around the floor to the tune of a Stevie Wonder hit *"Isn't She Lovely"*, with the necklace she had turned into a diamond and sapphire headband glittering in the candle-light. They were so in love it was almost embarrassing to watch the Royal couple…the Prince's pride in his glamorous young wife was obvious. (And following six pages)

Prince Charles scored a fine victory whilst playing polo at Werribee Park, Melbourne, and took the opportunity to kiss his wife, to the delight of the Australian crowd.

In November, 1985, the Prince and Princess of Wales visited The White House in Washington and were entertained by President Reagan and his wife, Nancy. Later, the Royal Couple attended a dinner in their honour, a much publicised star-spangled event staged in true American style. (Above and following four pages.)

Prince William, with his fellow pupils, on the way to a
school Christmas Nativity play in December 1985.

Prince Charles and Princess Diana took their January skiing holiday at Kloisters in Switzerland in 1986 – the same resort Charles had once taken Princess Diana's sister, Lady Sarah Spencer.

This is a rare glimpse into the private homelife of the Prince and Princess of Wales. These photographs, taken in the sunny first floor drawing room of their Kensington Palace home, reveal Diana's natural good taste in home decoration. The room's obvious warmth and style is a tribute to the Princess who chose all the furnishings and colour schemes for both her homes. The room is meant for a family to share and not just a little used sanctum to entertain guests. This is where Princes William and Harry come in the evenings for a final goodnight kiss from their parents. Few outsiders have been permitted into this private family world of the Royal couple.

In this photograph (Above) the Prince of Wales wears the full dress uniform of a Commander of the Royal Navy; in addition he wears the Order of the Garter sash, the Garter and Thistle Stars and the neck order of Grand Master of the Order of the Bath. His medals are the Queen's Service Order of New Zealand, the Jubilee Medal and the Coronation Medal. The Princess wears a cream duchess satin long evening dress with matching long-sleeved bolero a diamond and pearl drop tiara and diamond and pearl drop earrings. (Right) various studies of the Prince and Princess of Wales at Kensington Palace taken by Snowdon.

Both the Prince and Princess of Wales are fond of music and like to encourage Prince William and Prince Harry to familiarise themselves with the piano even at their early age. For the two young Princes, it is also another excuse for fun and games with Mummy and Daddy. The Royal parents insist on spending as much time as possible with their children, which has often meant re-scheduling official engagements so that they can both be back at home before the children's bedtime.

Above, Princess Diana spends a great deal of time playing with her children. She is seen here helping Prince William with his jigsaw puzzle. (Left) Prince Charles tries to lift Prince Henry onto the shoulders of Prince William, who seems to think it's great fun.

Rocking horses are the favourite toys (left) of Prince William and Henry in the playroom at Kensington Palace. (Above) Prince Henry's first steps, made on the 22nd of October 1985 with a little help from his older brother, Prince William, before launching out on his own.

This lovely family picture (right) was taken at Kensington Palace one month after the birth of Prince Henry on the 15th of September 1984. The Princess wore a cream satin with stand-up collar. Prince Charles, with his arms protectively round his wife and eldest son, was much less formally dressed. (Above) The Princess of Wales with her new-born baby and (left) Prince William hugs his little brother for the first time. (Overleaf) The Princess of Wales with young Prince Henry.

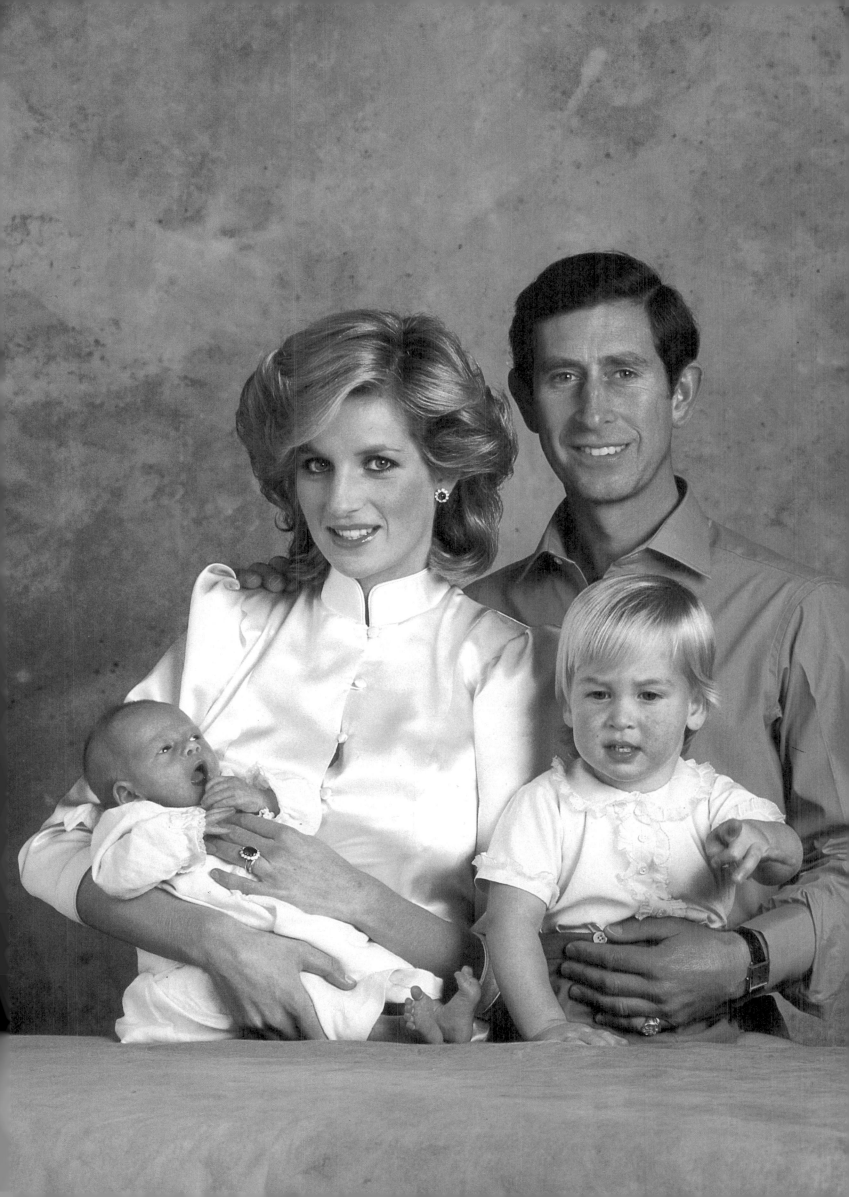

A very lively young Prince Henry photographed with his parents at their Kensington Palace home. Bringing up the children is the single most important job for the Prince and Princess of Wales, and they will be open-minded about the choice of schools. Both Prince Charles and Princess Diana love family life and the outdoors, and this is sure to influence the education their sons will receive. Certainly, it will not be easy for the young Princess, but they will be taught from an early age to fend for themselves. For the present, however, love and affection is what they need most.